Holiness

J.C. Ryle

Part 1

ISBN: 9798377208938

Revision 0 - 13-FEB-2023

Publisher: mmlj Publishing

Email: mmljPublishing@gmail.com

Holiness - Part 1

Chapter 1 - SIN

Chapter 2 - SANCTIFIED

Chapter 3 - HOLINESS

Green wording represents MMLJ Publishing update

~~Strikeout words represent prior Victorian wording~~

1 - SIN

"Everyone who sins also commits lawlessness.
Sin is lawlessness."

1 John 3:4

Whomever ~~He~~ wishes to attain understanding ~~views~~ about Christian holiness, must begin by examining the vast and sober ~~solemn~~ subject of sin. We ~~he~~ must dig down very low if we ~~he~~ would build high *(mmlj publishing: taller the building the deeper the foundation).* A mistake here is most harmful ~~mischievous~~.

Wrong views about holiness are generally traceable to wrong views about human corruption. I make no apology for beginning this volume of papers about holiness by making some plain statements about sin.

The plain truth is that a right knowledge of sin lies at the root of all saving Christianity. Without it such doctrines as justification, conversion, sanctification, are "words and names" which convey no meaning to the mind.

The first thing, therefore, that God does when He makes anyone a new creature in Christ, is to send light into their ~~his~~ heart, and show them ~~him~~ that they are ~~his is~~ a guilty sinner. The material creation in Genesis began with "light," and so also does the spiritual creation. God "shines into our hearts" by the work of the Holy Ghost, and then spiritual life begins. (2 Cor 4:6) - Dim or indistinct views of sin are the origin of most of the errors, opinions heresies, and false doctrines of the present day. If a person man does not realize the dangerous nature of their soul's disease, you cannot wonder if they are he content with false or imperfect medications. I believe that one of the main desires of the Church in the nineteenth century has been, and is, clearer, fuller teaching about sin.

I shall begin the subject by supplying some definition of sin. We are all of course familiar with the terms "sin" and "sinners." We talk frequently of "sin" being in the world, and of humans men ommitting "sins." But what do we mean by these terms and phrases? Do we really know? I fear there is much mental confusion and haziness on this point. Let me try, as briefly as possible, to supply an answer.

I say, then, that "sin," speaking generally, is, as the Ninth Article of our Church declares, "the fault and corruption of the nature of every human man that is naturally procreated engendered of the offspring of Adam; whereby humans are man is very far gone (quam longissime is the Latin) from original righteousness, and is of their his own nature inclined to evil, so that the flesh lusts always lusteth alway against the spirit; and, therefore, in every person born into the world, deserves it deserveth God's wrath and damnation." Sin, in short, is that vast moral disease which affects the whole human race, of every rank, and class, and name, and nation, and people, and tongue; a disease from which there never was but one born of woman that was free. Need I say that One was Christ Jesus the Lord?

I say, furthermore, that "a sin," to speak more particularly, consists in doing, saying, thinking, or imagining, anything that is not in perfect conformity with the mind and law of God. "Sin," in short, as the Scripture states saith, is "Everyone who sins also commits lawlessness. Sin is lawlessness."*(1 John 3:4)* ~~"the transgression of the law." (1 John iii. 4.)~~ The slightest outward or inward departure from absolute ~~mathematical~~ parallelism with God's revealed will and character constitutes a sin, and at once makes us guilty in God's sight.

Of course I need not tell any one who reads their ~~his~~ Bible with attention, that a person ~~man~~ may break God's law in heart and thought, when there is no overt and visible act of wickedness. Our Lord has settled that point beyond dispute in the Sermon on the Mount. *(Matt 5:21-28)* ~~(Matt. v. 21-28.)~~ Even a poet of our own has truly said, "A person ~~man~~ may smile and smile, and be a villain."

Again, I need not tell a careful student of the New Testament, that there are sins of omission as well as commission, and that we sin, as our Prayer-book justly reminds us, by "leaving undone the things we should have done ~~ought to do~~," as really as by "doing the things we should not have done ~~ought not to do~~." The dignified words of our Master in the Gospel of St. Matthew place this point also beyond dispute. It is there written, 'Depart from me, you cursed, into the eternal fire which is prepared for the devil and his angels; for I was hungry, and you didn't give me food to eat; I was thirsty, and you gave me no drink' *(Matt 25:41-42)* ~~"Depart, ye cursed, into everlasting fire: - for I was an hungered, and ye gave Me no meat; I was thirsty, and ye gave Me no drink." (Matt. xxv. 41, 42.)~~ It was a deep and thoughtful saying of holy Archbishop Usher, just before he died - ***"Lord, forgive me all my sins, and specially my sins of omission."***

But I do think it necessary in these times to remind my readers that a person ~~man~~ may commit sin and then ~~yet~~ be ignorant of it, and fancy themself ~~himself~~ innocent when they are ~~he is~~ guilty. I fail to see any Scriptural warrant for the modern assertion that "Sin is not sin to us until we detect ~~discern~~ it and are conscious of it." On the contrary, in the 4th and 5th chapters of that unduly neglected book, Leviticus, and in the 15th of Numbers, I find Israel distinctly taught that there were sins of ignorance which rendered people

unclean, and needed atonement. *(Leviticus 4:1-35; (Leviticus 5:14-19; Numbers 15:14-19)* ~~(Levit. iv. 1-35; v. 14-19; Num. xv. 25-29.)~~ And I find our Lord expressly teaching that "the servant who knew not their head of household ~~his master's~~ will and did it not," was not excused on account of his ignorance, but was "beaten" or punished. *(Luke 12:47)* ~~(Luke xii. 48.)~~ We shall do well to remember, that when we make our own miserably imperfect knowledge and consciousness the measure of our sinfulness, we are on very dangerous ground. A deeper study of Leviticus might do us much good.

Concerning the origin and source of this vast moral disease called "sin" I must say something. I fear the views of many professing Christians on this point are sadly defective and unsound. I dare not pass it by. Let us, then, have it fixed down in our minds that the sinfulness of a person ~~man~~ does not begin from without, but from within. It is not the result of bad training in early years. It is not picked up from bad companions and bad examples, as some weak Christians are too fond of saying. No! it is a family disease, which we all inherit from our first parents, Adam and Eve, and with which we are born. Created "in the image of God," innocent and righteous at first, our parents fell from original righteousness and became sinful and corrupt. And from that day to this all men and women are born in the image of fallen Adam and Eve, and inherit a heart and nature inclined to evil. "By one man sin entered into the world." - "That which is born of the flesh is flesh." - "We are by nature children of wrath." - "The earthly ~~carnal~~ mind is hostile ~~enmity~~ against God." - "For from within, out of the hearts, proceed evil thoughts, adulteries, sexual sins, murders, thefts" *(Matt 12:21)* ~~"Out of the heart (naturally as out of a fountain) proceed evil thoughts, adulteries,"~~ and the like. ~~(John iii. 6; Ephes. ii. 3; Rom. viii. 7; Mark vii. 21.)~~

The purist baby ~~fairest babe~~ that has entered life this year, and become the sunbeam of a family, is not, as its mother perhaps fondly calls it, a little "angel," or a little "innocent," but a little "sinner." So concerning ~~Alas!~~ as it lies smiling and crowing in its cradle, that little creature carries in its heart the seeds of every kind of wickedness! Only watch it carefully, as it grows in stature and its mind develops, and you will soon detect in it an incessant tendency to that which is bad, and a backwardness to that which is good. You will see in it the buds and germs of deceit, evil temper, selfishness, self-will, obstinacy, greediness, envy, jealousy, passion - which, if indulged and let alone, will shoot up with painful rapidity. Who taught the child these things? Where did they ~~he~~ learn them? The Bible alone can answer these questions!

Of all the foolish things that parents say about their children there is none worse than the common saying, "My child ~~son~~ has a good heart at the bottom. They are ~~He is~~ not what they ~~he~~ should ~~ought to~~ be; but they have ~~he has~~ fallen into bad hands. Public schools are bad places. The tutors neglect these children ~~the boys~~. Yet they have ~~he has~~ a good heart at the bottom." The truth, unhappily, is opposite ~~diametrically~~ the other way. The first cause of all sin lies in the natural corruption of the child's ~~boy's~~ own heart, and not in the school.

Concerning the extent of this vast moral disease of humans ~~man~~ called sin, let us beware that we make no mistake. The only safe ground is that which is laid for us in Scripture. **"God saw that the wickedness of man was great in the earth, and that every imagination of the thoughts of man's heart was continually only evil."** *(Genesis 6:5)* ; **"The heart is deceitful above all things and it is exceedingly corrupt."** *(Jeremiah 17:9)* ~~"Every imagination of the thoughts of his heart" is by nature "evil, and that continually." - "The heart is deceitful above all things, and desperately wicked," (Gen. vi. 5; Jer. xvii. 9.)~~

Sin is a disease which pervades and runs through every part of our moral constitution and every faculty of our minds. The understanding, the affections, the reasoning powers, the will, are all more or less infected. Even the conscience is so blinded that it cannot be depended on as a sure guide, and is as likely to lead people ~~men~~ wrong as right, unless it is enlightened by the Holy Ghost.

In short, "From the sole of the foot even to the head there is no soundness in it, but wounds, welts, and open sores." *(Isaiah 1:6)* ~~"from the sole of the foot even unto the head there is no soundness" about us. (Isa. i. 6.)~~ The disease may be veiled under a thin covering of courtesy, politeness, good manners, and outward decorum; but it lies deep down in the constitution.

I admit fully that humans have ~~man has~~ many grand and impressive abilities about themselves ~~noble faculties left about him~~, and that in arts and sciences and literature they ~~he~~ shows immense capacity. But the fact still remains that in spiritual things they are ~~he is~~ utterly "dead," and has no natural knowledge, or love, or fear of God. The ~~His~~ best things are so interwoven and intermingled with corruption, that the contrast only brings out into sharper relief the truth and extent of the fall. That one and the same creature should be in some things so high and in others so low

- so great and yet so little

- so lofty ~~noble~~ and yet so mean

- so grand in their ~~his~~ conception and execution of material things, and yet so shallow ~~grovelling~~ and corrupt ~~debased~~ in their ~~his~~ affections

- that they ~~he~~ should be able to plan and erect buildings like those to Carnac and Luxor in Egypt, and the Parthenon at Athens, and yet worship vile gods and goddesses, and birds, and beasts, and creeping things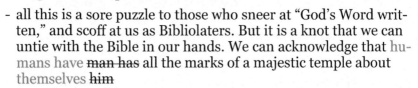

- that they ~~he~~ should be able to produce tragedies like those of Æschylus and Sophocles, and histories like that of Thucydides, and yet be a slave to abominable vices like those described in the first chapter of the Epistle to the Romans

- all this is a sore puzzle to those who sneer at "God's Word written," and scoff at us as Bibliolaters. But it is a knot that we can untie with the Bible in our hands. We can acknowledge that humans have ~~man has~~ all the marks of a majestic temple about themselves ~~him~~

- a temple in which God once dwelt, but a temple which is now in utter ruins

- a temple in which a shattered window here, and a doorway there, and a column there, still give some faint idea of the magnificence of the original design, but a temple which from end to end has lost its glory and fallen from its high estate. And we say that nothing solves the complicated problem of humans ~~man's~~ condition but the doctrine of original or birth-sin and the crushing effects of the fall.

Let us remember, besides this, that every part of the world bears testimony to the fact that sin is the universal disease of all humans ~~mankind~~. Search the globe from east to west and from pole to pole

- search every nation of every region ~~clime~~ in the four quarters of the earth

- search every rank and class in our own country from the highest to the lowest

- and under every circumstance and condition, the report will be always the same. The remotest islands in the Pacific Ocean, completely separate from Europe, Asia, Africa, and America, beyond the reach alike of Oriental luxury and Western arts and literature

- islands inhabited by people ignorant of books, money, steam, and gunpowder

- uncontaminated by the vices of modern civilization

- these very islands have always been found, when first discovered, the abode of the vilest forms of lust, cruelty, deceit, and superstition. If the inhabitants have known nothing else, they have always known how to sin! Everywhere the human heart is naturally *"**deceitful above all things, and desperately wicked.**"* *(Jeremiah 17:9)* ~~(Jer. xvii. 9.)~~

For my part, I know no stronger proof of the inspiration of Genesis and' the Mosaic account of the origin of humans ~~man~~, than the power, extent, and universality of sin. Grant that humans ~~mankind~~ have all sprung from one pair, and that this pair fell (as Gen. 3 tells us), and the state of human nature everywhere is easily accounted for. Deny it, as many do, and you are at once involved in inexplicable difficulties. In a word, the uniformity and universality of human corruption supply one of the most unanswerable instances of the enormous "difficulties of infidelity."

After all, I am convinced that the greatest proof of the extent and power of sin is the strong opinion pertinacity with which it divides cleaves to humans man even after they are he is converted and has become the subject of the Holy Ghost's operations. To use the language of the Ninth Article, "this infection of nature always doth remain - yet yea, even in them that are regenerate." So deeply planted are the roots of human corruption, that even after we are born again, renewed, "washed, sanctified, justified," and made living members of Christ, these roots remain alive in the bottom of our hearts, and, like the leprosy in the walls of the house, we never get rid of them until the earthly house of this tabernacle is dissolved.

Sin, no doubt, in the believer's heart, has no longer dominion. It is checked, controlled, mortified, and crucified by the expulsive power of the new principle of grace. The life of a believer is a life of victory, and not of failure. But the very struggles which go on within their body his bosom, the fight that they he finds it needful to fight

daily, the watchful jealousy which they are he is obliged to exercise over their his inner body man, the contest between the flesh and the spirit, the inward "groanings" which no one knows but they he who has experienced them - all, all testify to the same great truth, all show the enormous power and vitality of sin. Mighty indeed must that opponent foe be who even when crucified is still alive! Happy is that believer who understands it, and while they he rejoices in Christ Jesus has no confidence in the flesh; and while they say he says, "Thanks be unto God who gave giveth us the victory," never forgets to watch and pray they don't lest he fall into temptation!

Concerning the guilt, wickedness vileness, and offensiveness of sin in the sight of God, my words shall be few. I say "few" advisedly. I do not think, in the nature of things, that mortal humans man can at all realize the exceeding sinfulness of sin in the sight of that holy and perfect One with whom we have to do. On the one hand, God is that eternal Being who "charged chargeth His angels with foolishness folly," and in whose sight the very "heavens are not clean." He is One who reads thoughts and motives as well as actions, and requires "truth in the inward parts." *(Job 15:18) (Psalms 51:6)* ~~(Job xv. 18; xv. 15; Psa. li. 6.)~~

We, on the other hand - poor blind creatures, here today and gone tomorrow, born in sin, surrounded by sinners, living in a constant atmosphere of weakness, infirmity, and imperfection - can form none but the most inadequate conceptions of the hideousness of evil. We have no line to understand ~~fathom~~ it, and no measure by which to gauge it. The blind man can see no difference between a masterpiece of Titian or Raphael, and the Queen's Head on a village signboard. The deaf man cannot distinguish between a penny whistle and a cathedral organ. The very animals whose smell is most offensive to us have no idea that they are offensive, and are not offensive to one another. And human ~~man~~, fallen human ~~man~~, I believe, can have

no just idea what a vile thing sin is in the sight of that God whose handiwork is absolutely perfect

- perfect whether we look through telescope or microscope

- perfect in the formation of a mighty planet like Jupiter, with his satellites, keeping time to a second as he rolls round the sun

- perfect in the formation of the smallest insect that crawls over a foot of ground.

But let us nevertheless settle it firmly in our minds

- that sin is "***the abominable thing that God hates*** ~~hateth~~" *(Jeremiah 44:4)*

- that God "***is of purer eyes than to behold iniquity, and cannot look upon that which is evil***" *(Habakkuk 1:13)*

- that the least transgression of God's law makes us "***guilty of all***" *(James 2:10)*

- that "***the soul that sins*** ~~sinneth~~ ***shall die***" *(Ezekiel 18:4)*

- that "***the wages of sin is death***" *(Romans 6:12)*

- that God shall "***judge the secrets of humans*** ~~men~~" *(Romans 2:16)*

- that there is a ***worm that never dies, and a fire that is not quenched*** *(Mark 9:44)*

- that "***the wicked shall be turned into hell***" *(Pslams 9:17)*
- and "***shall go away into everlasting punishment***" *(Matthew 25:46)*
- and that "***nothing that defiles shall in any wise en-ter heaven.***" *(Revelation 21:27)*

~~(Jer. xliv. 4; Hab. i. 13; James ii. 10; Ezek. xviii. 4; Rom. vi. 23; Rom. ii. 16; Mark ix. 44; Ps. ix. 17; Matt. xxv. 46; Rev. xxi. 27.)~~

These are indeed tremendous words, when we consider that they are written in the Book of a most merciful God!

No proof of the fulness of sin, after all, is so overwhelming and unanswerable as the cross and passion of our Lord Jesus Christ, and the whole doctrine of His substitution and atonement. Terribly black must that guilt be for which nothing but the blood of the Son of God could make satisfaction. Heavy must that weight of human sin be which made Jesus groan and sweat drops of blood in agony at Gethsemane, and cry at Golgotha, "**My God, my God, why hast Thou forsaken Me?**" *(Matthew 27:46)* ~~(Matt. xxvii. 46.)~~

Nothing, I am convinced, will astonish us so much, when we awake in the resurrection day, as the view we shall have of sin, and the retrospect we shall take of our own countless shortcomings and defects. Never till the hour when Christ comes the second time shall we fully realize the "sinfulness of sin." Well might George Whitfield say, "The anthem in heaven will be, What possess ~~hath~~ God labor ~~wrought~~!"

One point only remains to be considered on the subject of sin, which I dare not pass over. That point is its ***deceitfulness***. It is a

point of most serious importance, and I venture to think it does not receive the attention which it deserves. You may see this deceitfulness in the wonderful proneness of humans ~~men~~ to regard sin as less sinful and dangerous than it is in the sight of God; and in their readiness to seem less offensive ~~extenuate it,~~ make excuses for it, and minimize its guilt.

- *"It is but a little one! God is merciful! God is not extreme to mark what is done amiss! We mean well! One cannot be so particular! Where is the mighty harm? We only do as others!"*

Who is not familiar with this kind of language?

- *You may see it in the long string of smooth words and phrases which* humans ~~men~~ *have coined in order to designate things which God calls downright wicked and ruinous to the soul. What do such expressions as "fast," "gay," "wild," "unsteady," "thoughtless," "loose" mean?*

They show that humans ~~men~~ try to cheat themselves into the belief that sin is not quite so sinful as God says it is, and that they are not so bad as they really are.

- *You may see it in the tendency even of believers to indulge their children in questionable practices, and to bind their own eyes to the inevitable result of the love of money, of tampering with temptation, and sanctioning a low standard of family religion.*

I fear we do not sufficiently realize the extreme delicateness ~~subtlety~~ of our soul's disease. We are too apt to forget that temptation to sin will rarely present itself to us in its true view ~~colours~~, saying, ***"I am your deadly enemy, and I want to ruin you for ever in hell."*** Oh, no! sin comes to us, like Judas, with a kiss; and like Joab, with an outstretched hand and flattering words. The forbidden fruit seemed good and desirable to Eve; yet it cast her out of Eden. The walking idly on his palace roof seemed harmless enough to David; yet it ended in adultery and murder.

Sin rarely seems sin at first beginnings. Let us then watch and pray, lest we fall into temptation. We may give wickedness smooth names, but we cannot alter its nature and character in the sight of God. Let us remember St. Paul's words: ***"Exhort one another daily, lest any be hardened through the deceitfulness of sin."*** *(Hebrews 3:13)* ~~(Heb. iii. 13.)~~ It is a wise prayer in our Litany,

"From the deceits of the world, the flesh, and the devil, good Lord, deliver us."

And now, before I go further, let me briefly mention two thoughts which appear to me to rise with irresistible force out of the subject.

On the one hand, I ask my readers to observe what deep reasons we all have for humiliation and self- abasement. Let us sit down before the picture of sin displayed to us in the Bible, and consider what guilty, vile, corrupt creatures we all are in the sight of God.

- What need we all have of that entire change of heart called re- generation, new birth, or conversion!

- What a mass of infirmity and imperfection cleaves to the very best of us at our very best!

-What an overwhelming thought it is, that **"without holiness no man shall see the Lord!"** *(Hebrews 12:14)* ~~(Heb. xii. 14.)~~

-What cause we have to cry with the publican, every night in our lives, when we think of our sins of omission as well as commission, **"God be merciful to me a sinner!"** *(Luke 18:13)* ~~(Luke xviii. 13.)~~

- How admirably suited are the general and Communion Confessions of the Prayer-book to the actual condition of all professing Christians! How well that language suits God's children which the Prayer-book puts in the mouth of every Churchman before they go ~~he goes~~ up to the Communion Table

- "The remembrance of our misdoings is grievous unto us; the burden is intolerable. Have mercy upon us, have mercy upon us, most merciful Father; for Thy Son our Lord Jesus Christ's sake, forgive us all that is past."

- How true it is that **"the holiest saint is in himself a miserable sinner,"** and a debtor to mercy and grace to the last moment of his existence!

With my whole heart I subscribe to that passage in Hooker's sermon on Justification, which begins, "Let the holiest and best things we do be considered. We are never better affected unto God than when we pray; yet when we pray, how are our affections many times distracted!

- How little reverence do we show unto the grand majesty of God unto whom we speak I How little remorse of our own miseries!

- How little taste of the sweet influence of His tender mercies do we feel! Are we not as unwilling many times to begin, and as glad to make an end, as if in saying, 'Call upon Me,'

- He had set us a very burdensome task? It may seem somewhat extreme, which I will speak; therefore, let every one judge of it, even as his own heart shall tell him, and not otherwise; I will but only make a demand!

- If God should yield unto us, not as unto Abraham - If fifty, forty, thirty, twenty - yea, or if ten good persons could be found in a city, for their sakes this city should not be destroyed;

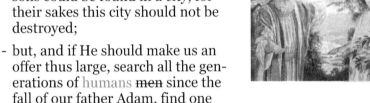

- but, and if He should make us an offer thus large, search all the generations of humans ~~men~~ since the fall of our father Adam, find one man that hath done one action which has ~~hath~~ passed from him pure, without any stain or blemish at all;

- and for that one humans ~~man's~~ only action neither humans ~~man~~ nor angel should feel the torments which are prepared for both.

Do you think that this ransom to deliver men and angels could be found to be among the sons of men? The best things which we do have somewhat in them to be pardoned. "

That witness is true. For my part I am persuaded the more light we have, the more we see our own sinfulness: the nearer we get to heaven, the more we are clothed with humility.

In every age of the Church you will find it true, if you will study biographies, that the most eminent saints - men like Bradford, Rutherford, and McCheyne - ***have always been the humblest men***.

On the other hand, I ask my readers to observe how deeply thankful we ought to be for the glorious Gospel of the grace of God.

There is a remedy revealed for man's need, as wide and broad and deep as man's disease. We need not be afraid to look at sin, and study its nature, origin, power, extent, and vileness, if we only look at the same time at the Almighty medicine provided for us in the salvation that is in Jesus Christ. Though sin has abounded, grace has <u>much more abounded</u>. Yes: in the everlasting covenant of redemption, to which Father, Son, and Holy Ghost are parties

- in the Mediator of that covenant, Jesus Christ the righteous, perfect God and perfect Man in one Person

- in the work that He did by dying for our sins and rising again for our justification

- in the offices that He fills as our Priest, Substitute, Physician, Shepherd, and Advocate

- in the precious blood He shed which can cleanse from all sin

- in the everlasting righteousness that He brought in

- in the perpetual intercession that He carries on as our Representative at God's right hand

- in His power to save to the uttermost the chief of sinners, His willingness to receive and pardon the vilest, His readiness to bear with the weakest

- in the grace of the Holy Spirit which He plants in the hearts of all His people, renewing, sanctifying and causing old things to pass away and all things to become new

- in all this - and oh, what a brief sketch it is!

- in all this, I say, ***there is a full, perfect, and complete medicine for the hideous disease of sin***.

Awful and tremendous as the right view of sin undoubtedly is, no

one need faint and despair if they he will take a right view of Jesus Christ at the same time. No wonder that old Flavel (tug boat captain) ends many a chapter of his admirable "Fountain of Life" with the touching words, "Blessed be God for Jesus Christ."

In bringing this mighty subject to a close, I feel that I have only touched the surface of it. It is one which cannot be thoroughly handled in a paper like this. They He that would see it treated fully and exhaustively must turn to such masters of experimental theology as Owen, and Burgess, and Manton, and Charnock, and the other giants of the Puritan school. On subjects like this there are no writers to be compared to the Puritans. It only remains for me to point out some practical uses to which the whole doctrine of sin may be profitably turned in the present day.

I say, then, in the first place, that a Scriptural view of sin ~~ski~~ is one of the best antidotes to that vague, dim, misty, hazy kind of theology which is so painfully current in the present age. It is vain to shut our eyes to the fact that there is a vast quantity of so-called Christianity now-a-days which you cannot declare positively unsound, but which, nevertheless, is not full measure, good weight, and sixteen ounces to the pound. It is a Christianity in which there is undeniably

"something about Christ, and something about grace, and something about faith, and something about repentance, and something about holiness";

but it is not the real "thing as it is" in the Bible. Things are out of place, and out of proportion. As old Latimer would have said, it is a kind of "mingle-mangle," and does no good. It neither exercises influence on daily conduct, nor comforts in life, nor gives peace in death; and those who hold it often awake too late to find that they have got nothing solid under their feet. Now I believe the likeliest way to cure and mend this defective kind of religion is to bring forward more prominently the old Scriptural truth about the sinfulness of sin. People will never set their faces decidedly towards heaven, and live like pilgrims, until they really feel that they are in danger of hell.

Let us all try to revive the old teaching about sin, in nurseries, in schools, in training colleges, in Universities. Let us not forget that "**the law is good if we use it lawfully,**" and that ' **by the law is the knowledge of sin.**" *(1 Timothy 1:8) (Romans 3:20) (Romans 7:7)* ~~(1 Tim. i. 8; Rom. iii. 20; vii. 7.)~~

Let us bring the law to the front and press it on men's attention. Let us expound and beat out the Ten Commandments, and show the length, and width ~~breadth~~, and depth, and height of their requirements. This is the way of our Lord in the Sermon on the Mount. We cannot do better than follow His plan. We may depend upon it, men will never come to Jesus, and stay with Jesus, and live for Jesus, unless they really know why they are to come, and what is their need. Those whom the Spirit draws to Jesus are those whom the Spirit has convinced of sin. Without thorough conviction of sin, men may seem to come to Jesus and follow Him for a season, but they will soon fall away and return to the world.

In the next place, a Scriptural view of sin is one of the best antidotes to the extravagantly broad and liberal theology which is so much in vogue at the present time. ***The tendency of modern thought is to reject dogmas, creeds, and every kind of bounds in religion.*** It is thought grand and wise to condemn no opinion whatsoever, and to pronounce all earnest and clever teachers to be trustworthy, however diverse in character ~~heterogeneous~~ and mutually destructive their opinions may be.

- Everything indeed ~~forsooth~~ is true, and nothing is false! Everybody is right, and nobody is wrong! Everybody is likely to be saved, and nobody is to be lost!

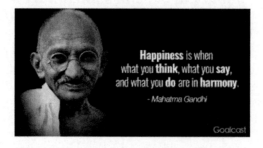

- The Atonement and Substitution of Christ, the personality of the devil, the miraculous element in Scripture, the reality and eternity of future punishment, all these mighty foundation-stones are coolly tossed overboard, like lumber, in order to lighten the ship of Christianity, and enable it to keep pace with modern science.

- Stand up for these great verities, and you are called narrow, illiberal, old-fashioned, and a theological fossil! Quote a text, and you are told that all truth is not confined to the pages of an ancient Jewish Book, and that free inquiry has found out many things since the Book was completed!

Now, I know nothing so likely to counteract this modern plague as constant clear statements about the nature, reality, vileness, power, and guilt of sin. We must charge home into the consciences of these human ~~men~~ of broad views, and demand a plain answer to some plain questions.

We must ask them to lay their hands on their hearts, and tell us whether their favorite ~~favourite~~ opinions comfort them in the day of sickness, in the hour of death, by the bedside of dying parents, by the grave of beloved wife or child.

We must ask them whether a vague earnestness, without definite doctrine, gives them peace at seasons like these.

We must challenge them to tell us whether they do not sometimes feel a gnawing "something" within, which all the free inquiry and philosophy and science in the world cannot satisfy.

And then we must tell them that this gnawing "something" is the sense of sin, guilt, and corruption, which they are leaving out in their calculations. And, above all, we must tell them that nothing will ever make them feel rest, but submission to the old doctrines of man's ruin and Christ's redemption, and simple childlike faith in Jesus.

In the next place, a right view of sin is the best antidote to that sensuous, ceremonial, formal kind of Christianity, which has swept over England like a flood in the last twenty-five years, and carried away so many before it. I can well believe that there is much that is attractive in this system of religion, to a certain order of minds, so long as the conscience is not fully enlightened. But when that wonderful part of our constitution called conscience is really awake and alive, I find it hard to believe that a pleasing ~~sensuous~~ ceremonial Christianity will thoroughly satisfy us.

A little child is easily quieted and amused with gaudy toys, and dolls, and rattles, so long as it is not hungry; but once let it feel the cravings of nature within, and we know that nothing will satisfy it but food. Just so it is with man in the matter of his soul. Music, and flowers, and candles, and incense, and banners, and processions, and beautiful vestments, and confessionals, and man-made ceremonies of a semi-Romish character, may do well enough for him under certain conditions. But once let him "***awake and arise from the dead,***" and they ~~he~~ will not rest content with these things. They will seem to ~~him~~ them no more formal importance ~~mere solemn triflings~~, and a waste of time. Once let they ~~him~~ see their ~~his~~ sin, and they ~~he~~ must see his Savior ~~Saviour~~. They ~~He~~ feels stricken with a deadly disease, and nothing will satisfy them ~~him~~ but the great Physician. Their ~~He~~ hungers and thirsts, and they ~~he~~ must have nothing less than the bread of life. I may seem bold in what I am about to say; but I fearlessly venture the assertion, that four-fifths of the semi-Romanism of the last quarter of a century would never have existed if English people had been taught more fully and clearly the nature, vileness, and sinfulness of sin.

In the next place, a right view of sin is one of the best antidotes to the overstrained theories of Perfection, of which we hear so much in these times. I shall say but little about this, and in saying it I trust I shall not give offense ~~offence~~. If those who press on us perfection mean nothing more than an all-round consistency, and a careful attention to all the graces which make up the Christian character, reason would  that we should not only bear with them, but agree with them entirely. By all means let us aim high.

- But if humans ~~men~~ really mean to tell us that here in this world a believer can attain to entire freedom from sin, live for years in unbroken and uninterrupted communion with God, and feel for months together not so much as one evil thought, I must honestly say that such an opinion appears to me very unscriptural.

- I go even further. I say that the opinion is very dangerous to them ~~him~~ that holds it, and very likely to depress, discourage, and keep back inquirers after salvation. ***I cannot find the slightest warrant in God's Word for expecting such perfection as this while we are in the body.*** I believe the words of our Fifteenth Article are strictly true

- that *"Christ alone is without sin; and that all we, the rest, though baptized and born again in Christ, offend in many things; and if we say that we have no sin, we deceive ourselves, and the truth is not in us."*

- To use the language of our first Homily, *"There be imperfections in our best works: we do not love God so much as we are bound to do, with all our hearts, mind, and power; we do not fear God so much as we ought to do; we do not pray to God but with many and great imperfections. We give, forgive, believe, live, and hope imperfectly; we speak, think, and do imperfectly; we fight against the devil, the world, and the flesh imperfectly. Let us, therefore, not be ashamed to confess plainly our state of imperfections."*

- Once more I repeat what I have said, the best preservative against this temporary delusion about perfection which clouds some minds

- for such I hope I may call it

- is a clear, full, distinct understanding of the nature, sinfulness, and deceitfulness of sin.

In the last place, a Scriptural view of sin will prove an admirable antidote to them low views of personal holiness which are so painfully prevalent in these last days of the Church. **This is a very painful and delicate subject,** I know; but I dare not turn away from it. It has long been my sorrowful conviction that the

standard of daily life among professing Christians in this country has been gradually falling. I am afraid that Christ-like charity, kindness, good-temper, unselfishness, meekness, gentleness, good-nature, self-denial, zeal to do good, and separation from the world, are far less appreciated than they ought to be, and than they used to be in the days of our fathers.

Into the causes of this state of things I cannot pretend to enter fully, and can only suggest conjectures for consideration. It may be that a certain profession of religion has become so fashionable and comparatively easy in the present age, that the streams which were once narrow and deep have become wide and shallow, and what we have gained in outward show we have lost in quality. It may be that the vast increase of wealth in the last twenty-five years has insensibly introduced a plague of worldliness, and self-indulgence, and love of ease into social life.

> *What were once called luxuries are now comforts and necessaries, and self-denial and "enduring hardness" are consequently little known. It may be that the enormous amount of controversy which marks this age has insensibly dried up our spiritual life.*

We have too often been content with zeal for orthodoxy, and have neglected the sober realities of daily practical godliness. Be the causes what they may, I must declare my own belief that the result remains.

> *There has been of late years a lower standard of personal holiness among believers than there used to be in the days of our fathers. The whole result is that the spirit is grieved! and the matter calls for much humiliation and searching of heart.*

As to the best remedy for the state of things I have mentioned, I shall venture to give an opinion. Other schools of thought in the Churches must judge for themselves. The cure for Evangelical Churchmen, I am convinced, is to be found in a clearer apprehension of the nature and sinfulness of sin. **We need not go back to Egypt,** and borrow semi-Romish practices in order to revive our spiritual life. **We need not restore the confessional, or return to monasticism or asceticism.** Nothing of the kind!

We must simply repent and do our first works. We must return to first principles. We must go back to "the old paths." We must sit down humbly in the presence of God, look the whole subject in the face, examine clearly what the Lord Jesus calls sin, and what the Lord Jesus calls "doing His will."

We must then try to realize that it is terribly possible to live a careless, easy-going, half-worldly life, and yet at

the same time to maintain Evangelical principles and call ourselves Evangelical people!

Once let us see that sin is far extremely unpleasant ~~viler~~, and far nearer to us, and sticks more closely to us than we supposed, and we shall be led, I trust and believe, to get nearer to Christ. Once drawn nearer to Christ, we shall drink more deeply out of His fullness, and learn more thoroughly to "***live the life of faith***" in Him, as St. Paul did.

Once taught to live the life of faith in Jesus, and abiding in Him, we shall bear more fruit, shall find ourselves more strong for duty, more patient in trial, more watchful over our poor weak hearts, and more like our Master in all our little daily ways. Just in proportion as we realize how much Christ has done for us, shall we labor ~~labour~~ to do much for Christ. Much forgiven, we shall love much. In short, as the Apostle says, "***with open face beholding as in a glass the glory of the Lord, we are changed into the same image even as by the Spirit of the Lord.***" *(2 Timothy 3:18)* ~~(2 Cor. iii. 18.)~~

Whatever some may please to think or say, there can be no doubt that an increased feeling about holiness is one of the signs of the times. Conferences for the promotion of "spiritual life" are becoming common in the present day. The subject of "spiritual life" finds a place on Congress platforms almost every year. It has awakened an amount of interest and general attention throughout the land, for which we ought to be thankful.

An movement, based on sound principles, which helps to deepen our spiritual life and increase our personal holiness, will be a real blessing to the Church of England. It will do much to draw us together and heal our unhappy divisions. It may bring down some fresh out-pouring of the grace of the Spirit, and be "life from the dead" in these later times. But sure I am, as I said in the beginning of this paper,

> ***we must begin low, if we would build high, I am convinced that the first step towards attaining a higher standard of holiness is to realize more fully the amazing sinfulness of sin.***

2 - SANCTIFICATION

"Sanctify them in your truth. Your word is truth."

1 John 3:4

" "Sanctify them through Thy truth." - John xvii. 17.

"For this is the will of God: your sanctification, that you abstain from sexual immorality, that each one of you know how to control his own body in sanctification and honor, not in the passion of lust, even as the Gentiles who don't know God"

1 Thessalonians 4:3-5

"This is the will of God, even jour sanctification." - 1 Thess. iv. 3.

The subject of sanctification is one which many, I fear, dislike exceedingly. Some even turn from it with scorn and disdain. The very last thing they would like is to be a "saint," or a "sanctified" person man. Yet the subject does not deserve to be treated in this way. It is not an enemy, but a friend.

It is a subject of the utmost importance to our souls. If the Bible be true, it is certain that unless we are "sanctified," we shall not be saved.

There are three things which, according to the Bible, are absolutely necessary to the salvation of

every man and woman in Christendom. These three are, justification, regeneration, and sanctification. All three meet in every child of God: they are ~~he is~~ **both born again, and justified, and sanctified.** If they lack ~~He that lacks~~ **any one of these three things is not a true Christian in the sight of God, and dying in that condition will not be found in heaven and glorified in the last day.**

It is a subject which is especially ~~peculiarly~~ appropriate ~~seasonable~~ in the present day. Strange doctrines have risen up of late upon the whole subject of sanctification. Some appear to confuse ~~confound~~ it with justification. Others waste ~~fritter~~ it away to nothing, under the pretense ~~pretence~~ of zeal for free grace, and practically neglect it altogether. Others are so much afraid of "works" being made a part of justification, that they can hardly find any place at all for "works" in their religion. Others set up a wrong standard of sanctification before their eyes, and failing to attain it, waste their lives in repeated membership ~~secessions~~ from church to church, chapel to chapel, and sect to sect, in the vain hope that they will find what they want. In a day like this, a calm examination of the subject, as a great leading doctrine of the Gospel, may be of great use to our souls.

Let us consider, firstly, the true nature of sanctification.

Let us consider, secondly, the visible marks of sanctification.

Let us consider, lastly, wherein justification and sanctification agree and are like one another, and wherein they differ and are unlike.

<u>If, unhappily, the reader of these pages is one of those who care for nothing but this world, and make no profession of religion, I cannot expect him to take much interest in what I am writing.</u> You will probably think it an affair of "words, and names," and nice questions, about which it matters nothing what you hold and believe. ***But if you are a thoughtful, reasonable, sensible Christian, I venture to say that you will find it worth while to have some clear ideas about sanctification.***

In the first place, we have to consider the nature of sanctification. What does the Bible mean when it speaks of a "sanctified" man?

Sanctification is that inward spiritual work which the Lord Jesus Christ works in a man by the Holy Ghost, when He calls him to be a true believer.

> **He not only washes him from his sins in His own blood, but He also separates him from his natural love of sin and the world, puts a new principle in his heart, and makes him practically godly in life.**

The instrument by which the Spirit effects this work is generally the Word of God, though **He sometimes uses afflictions and providential visitations "without the Word."** *(1 Peter 3:1)* ~~(1 Peter iii. 1.)~~ The subject of this work of Christ by His Spirit is called in Scripture a "sanctified" man.

> **He who supposes that Jesus Christ only lived and died and rose again in order to provide justification and forgiveness of sins for His people, has yet much to learn.**

Whether they ~~he~~ knows it or not, they are ~~he is~~ dishonoring ~~dishonouring~~ our blessed Lord, and making Him only a half Savior ~~Saviour~~. The Lord Jesus has undertaken everything that His people's souls require; not only to deliver them from the guilt of their sins by His atoning death, but from the dominion of their sins, by placing in their hearts the Holy Spirit; not only to justify them, but also to sanctify them. He is, thus, not only their "righteousness," but their "sanctification." *(1 Corinthians 1:30)* ~~(1 Cor. i. 30.)~~

Let us hear what the Bible says: "For their sakes I sanctify myself, that they also might be sanctified." *(John 17:19)*

- "Christ loved the Church, and gave Himself for it; that He might sanctify and cleanse it." *(Ephesians 5:25)*

- "Christ gave Himself for us, that He might redeem us from all iniquity, and purify unto Himself a peculiar people, zealous of good works." *(Titus 2;14)*

- "Christ bore our sins in His own body on the tree, that we, being dead to sins, should live unto righteousness." *(1 Peter 2:24)*

- "Christ hath reconciled (you) in the body of His flesh through death, to present you holy and unblameable and unreproveable in His sight." *(1 Peter 2:24).*

    ~~(John xvii. 19; Ephes. v. 25; Titus ii. 14; 1 Peter ii. 24; Coloss. i. 22.)~~

Let the meaning of these five texts be carefully considered. If words mean anything, they teach that Christ undertakes the sanctification, no less than the justification of His believing people. Both are alike provided for in that "everlasting covenant ordered in all things and sure," of which the Mediator is Christ. In fact, Christ in one place is called "He that sanctifieth," and His People, "they who are sanctified." *(Hebrew 2:11)* ~~(Heb. ii. 11.)~~

The subject before us is of such deep and vast importance, that it requires fencing, guarding, clearing up, and marking out on every side.

A doctrine which is needful to salvation can never be too sharply developed, or brought too fully into light. To clear away the confusion between doctrines and doctrines, which is so unhappily common among Christians, and to map out the precise relation between truths and truths in religion, is one way to attain accuracy in our theology. I shall therefore not hesitate to lay before my readers a series of connected propositions or statements, drawn from Scripture, which I think will be found useful in defining the exact nature of sanctification.

Sanctification, then, is the invariable result of that vital union with Christ which true faith gives to a Christian.

- **"I am the vine. You are the branches. He who remains in me and I in him bears much fruit, for apart from me you can do nothing"** *(John 15:5).* ~~He that abideth in Me, and I in him, the same bringeth forth much fruit." (John xv. 5.)~~

- The branch which bears no fruit is no living branch of the vine. The union with Christ which produces no effect on heart and life is a mere formal union, which is worthless before God. The faith which has not a sanctifying influence on the character is no better than the faith of devils. It is a "dead faith, because it is alone." It is not the gift of God. It is not the faith of God's elect.

In short, where there is no sanctification of life, there is no real faith in Christ. True faith works ~~worketh~~ by love. In constrains a person ~~man~~ to live unto the Lord from a deep sense of gratitude for redemption. It makes them ~~him~~ feel that they ~~he~~ can never do too much for Him that died for him. Being much forgiven, they ~~he~~ loves much. They ~~He~~ whom the blood cleanses, walks in the light. They ~~He~~ who have ~~has~~ real lively hope in Christ, purifies themselves ~~purifieth himself~~ even as He is pure.

- "Even so faith, if it has no works, is dead in itself. Yes, a man will say, "You have faith, and I have works." Show me your faith

without works, and I will show you my faith by my works. You believe that God is one. You do well. The demons also believe—and shudder. But do you want to know, vain man, that faith apart from works is dead?" *(James 2:17-20)*

-"Paul, a servant of God and an apostle of Jesus Christ, according to the faith of God's chosen ones and the knowledge of the truth which is according to godliness" *(Titus 1:1)*

- "For in Christ Jesus neither circumcision nor uncircumcision amounts to anything, but faith working through love" *(Galatians 5:6)*

- "But if we walk in the light as he is in the light, we have fellowship with one another, and the blood of Jesus Christ his Son, cleanses us from all sin" *(1 John 1:7)*

- "Everyone who has this hope set on him purifies himself, even as he is pure" *(1 John 3:3)*

~~(James ii. 17-20; Titus i. 1; Gal. v. 6; 1 John i. 7; iii. 3.). (ohn 15:5).~~

Sanctification, again, is the outcome and inseparable consequence of regeneration. They are ~~He that is~~ born again and made a new creature, receives a new nature

and a new principle, and always lives a new life. A regeneration which a person **man can have, and yet live carelessly in sin or worldliness, is a regeneration invented by uninspired theologians, but never mentioned in Scripture.**

On the contrary, St. John expressly says, that

- "If you know that he is righteous, you know that everyone who practices righteousness has been born of him" *(1 John 2:29)*

- "Whoever is born of God doesn't commit sin, because his seed remains in him, and he can't sin, because he is born of God. In this the children of God are revealed, and the children of the devil. Whoever doesn't do righteousness is not of God, neither is he who doesn't love his brother. For this is the message which you heard from the beginning, that we should love one another — unlike Cain, who was of the evil one and killed his brother. Why did he kill him? Because his deeds were evil, and his brother's righteous. Don't be surprised, my brothers, if the world hates you. We know that we have passed out of death into life, because we love the brothers. He who doesn't love his brother remains in death." *(1 John 3:9-14)*

- "For whatever is born of God overcomes the world. This is the victory that has overcome the world: your faith. Who is he who overcomes the world, but he who believes that Jesus is the Son of God?

    - This is he who came by water and blood, Jesus Christ; not with the water only, but with the water and the blood. It is the Spirit who testifies, because the Spirit is the truth. For there are three who testify: the Spirit, the water, and the blood; and the three agree as one.

    - If we receive the witness of men, the witness of God is greater; for this is God's testimony which he has testified concerning his Son.

    - He who believes in the Son of God has the testimony in himself. He who doesn't believe God has made him a liar, because he has not believed in the testimony that God has given concerning his Son.

- The testimony is this: that God gave to us eternal life, and this life is in his Son.

- He who has the Son has the life. He who doesn't have God's Son doesn't have the life.

- These things I have written to you who believe in the name of the Son of God, that you may know that you have eternal life, and that you may continue to believe in the name of the Son of God.

- This is the boldness which we have toward him, that if we ask anything according to his will, he listens to us.

- And if we know that he listens to us, whatever we ask, we know that we have the petitions which we have asked of him.

- If anyone sees his brother sinning a sin not leading to death, he shall ask, and God will give him life for those who sin not leading to death. There is sin leading to death. I don't say that he should make a request concerning this.

- All unrighteousness is sin, and there is sin not leading to death.

- We know that whoever is born of God doesn't sin, but he who was born of God keeps himself, and the evil one doesn't touch him." *(1 John 5:4-18)*

-"He that is born of God doth not commit sin - doeth righteousness - loveth the brethren - keepeth himself - and overcometh the world." (1 John ii. 29; iii. 9-14; v. 4-18.)

In a word, where there is no sanctification there is no regeneration, and where there is no holy life there is no new birth. This is, no doubt, a hard saying to many minds; but, hard or not, it is simple Bible truth.

It is written plainly, that whom he who is born of God is one whose "Whoever is born of God doesn't commit sin, because his seed remains in him, and he can't sin, because he is born of God." seed remaineth in him, and he cannot sin, because he is born of God." *(1 John 3:9)* (1 John iii. 9.)

Sanctification, again, is the only certain evidence of that in-dwelling of the Holy Spirit which is essential to salvation. "**If any man have not the Spirit of Christ, he is none of His.**" *(Romans 8:9)* (Rom. viii. 9.)

The Spirit never lies dormant and idle within the soul: They He always makes His presence known by the fruit He causes to be borne in heart, character, and life. "**The fruit of the Spirit**," says St. Paul, "**is love, joy, peace, long- suffering, gentleness, goodness, faith, meekness, temperance**," and such like. *(Galatians 5:22)* (Gal. v. 22.)

Where these things are to be found, there is the Spirit: where these things are wanting, people men are dead before God. The Spirit is compared to the wind, and, like the wind, He cannot be seen by our bodily eyes. But just as we know there is a wind by the effect it produces on waves, and trees, and smoke, so we may know the Spirit is in a person man by the effects He produces in the persons man's conduct. It is nonsense to suppose that we have the Spirit, if we do not also "walk in the Spirit." *(Galatians 5:25)* (Gal. v. 25.)

<u>We may depend on it as a positive certainty, that where there is no holy living, there is no Holy Ghost.</u> The seal that the Spirit stamps on Christ's people is sanctification. As many as are actually "led by the Spirit of God, they," and they only, "are the sons of God." *(Romans 8:14)* (Rom. viii. 14.)

Sanctification, again, is the only sure mark of God's election. The names and number of the elect are a secret thing, no doubt, which God has wisely kept in His own power, and not revealed to humans man. It is not given to us in this world to study the pages of the book of life, and see if our names are there. But if there is one thing clearly and plainly laid down about election, it is this

- that elect men and women may be known and distinguished by holy lives. It is expressly written that they are "elect through sanctification

- chosen unto salvation through sanctification

- predestinated to be conformed to the image of God's Son

- and chosen in Christ before the foundation of the world that they should be holy."

Hence, when St. Paul saw the working "faith" and labor ~~laboring~~ "love" and patient "hope" of the Thessalonian believers, he says, "I know your election of God." *(1 Peter 1:2; 2 Thessalonians 2:13, Ephesians 1:4; 1 Thessalonians 1:3-4)* ~~(1 Peter i. 2; 2 Thess. ii. 13; Rom. viii. 29; Eph. i. 4; 1 Thess. i. 3, 4.)~~

They whom ~~He that~~ boasts of being one of God's elect, while they are ~~he is~~ willfully and habitually living in sin, is only deceiving himself, and talking wicked blasphemy.

Of course it is hard to know what people really are, and many who make a fair show outwardly in religion, may turn out at last to be rotten-hearted hypocrites. But where there is not, at least, some appearance of sanctification, we may be quite certain there is no election. The Church Catechism correctly and wisely teaches that the Holy Ghost "sanctifieth all the elect people of God."

Sanctification, again, is a thing that will always be seen. Like the Great Head of the Church, from whom it springs, it ***"cannot be hid." "Every tree is known by his own fruit."*** *(Luke 6:44)* ~~(Luke vi. 44.)~~

A truly sanctified person may be so clothed with humility, that they ~~he~~ can see in themselves ~~himself~~ nothing but infirmity and defects.

Like Moses, when he came down from the Mount, he may not be conscious that his face shines.

Like the righteous, in the mighty parable of the sheep and the goats, he may not see that he has done anything worthy of his Master's notice and commendation: **"Then the righteous will answer him, saying, 'Lord, when did we see you hungry**

and feed you, or thirsty and give you a drink?" *(Matthew 25:37)* ~~"When saw we Thee an hungered, and fed Thee?" (Matt. xxv. 37.)~~

But whether they see it themselves ~~he sees it himself~~ or not, others will always see in them ~~him~~ a tone, and taste, and character, and habit of life unlike that of other people ~~men~~. The very idea of a person ~~man~~ being "sanctified," while no holiness can be seen in their ~~his~~ life, <u>is flat nonsense and a misuse of words.</u>

> *Light may be very dim; but if there is only a spark in a dark room it will be seen.*
>
> *Life may be very feeble; but if the pulse only beats a little, it will be felt.*

It is just the same with a sanctified person ~~man~~: their ~~his~~ sanctification will be something felt and seen, though they ~~he himself~~ may not understand it.

A "saint" in whom nothing can be seen but worldliness or sin, is a kind of monster not recognized ~~recognised~~ **in the Bible!**

Sanctification, again, is a thing for which every believer is responsible. In saying this I would not be mistaken. I hold as strongly as anyone that <u>every person ~~man~~ on earth is accountable to God</u>, and that all the lost will be speechless and without excuse at the last day. Every person ~~man~~ has power to "***lose his own soul.***" *(Matthew 16:26)* ~~(Matt. xvi. 26.)~~

But while I hold this, I maintain that believers are eminently and peculiarly responsible, and under a special obligation to live holy lives. They are not as others, dead and blind and un-renewed: <u>they are alive unto God, and have light and knowledge, and a new principle within them.</u>

- Whose fault is it if they are not holy, but their own?

- On whom can they throw the blame if they are not sanctified, but themselves?

God, who has given them grace and a new heart, and a new nature, has deprived them of all excuse if they do not live for His praise. This is a point which is far too much forgotten.

A person ~~man~~ who professes to be a true Christian, while they ~~he~~ sits still, content with a very low degree of sanctification (if indeed they have ~~he has~~ any at all), and coolly tells you they ~~he~~ "can do nothing," is a very pitiable sight, and a very ignorant person ~~man~~.

Against this delusion let us watch and be on our guard. The Word of God always addresses its precepts to believers as accountable and responsible beings. If the savior ~~Saviour~~ of sinners gives us renewing grace, and calls us by His Spirit, we may be sure that He <u>expects us to use our grace, and not to go to sleep.</u>

It is forgetfulness of this which causes many believers to "grieve the Holy Spirit," and makes them very useless and uncomfortable Christians.

Sanctification, again, is a thing which admits of growth and degrees. A person ~~man~~ may climb from one step to another in holiness, and be far more sanctified at one period of their ~~his~~ life than another. More pardoned and more justified than they are ~~he is~~ when they ~~he~~ first believes, they ~~he~~ cannot be, though they ~~he~~ may feel it more. More sanctified than they ~~he~~ certainly may be, because every grace in their ~~his~~ new character may be strengthened, enlarged, and deepened. This is the evident meaning of our Lord's last prayer for His disciples, when He used the words,

-"Sanctify them in your truth. Your word is truth." ~~"Sanctify them"~~ *(John 17:17)*

-and of St. Paul's prayer for the Thessalonians, "For this is the will of God: your sanctification, that you abstain from sexual immorality, that each one of you know how to control his own body in sanctification and honor," *(1 Thessalonians 4:3-4)* ~~"The very God of peace sanctify you." (John xvii. 17; 1 Thess. iv. 3.)~~

In both cases the expression plainly implies the possibility of increased sanctification; while such an expression as <u>"justify them"</u>

is never once in Scripture applied to a believer, because they ~~he~~ cannot be more justified than he is.

I can find no warrant in Scripture for the doctrine of "imputed sanctification." It is a doctrine which seems to me to confuse things that differ, and to lead to very evil consequences. Not least, it is a doctrine which is flatly contradicted by the experience of all the most eminent Christians. If there is any point on which God's holiest saints agree it is this: that they see more, and know more, and feel more, and do more, and repent more, and believe more, as they get on in spiritual life, and in proportion to the closeness of their walk with God.

In short, they **"grow in grace,"** as St. Peter exhorts believers to do; and **"abound more and more,"** ac cording to the words of St. Paul. *(2 Peter 3:18) (1 Thessalonians 4:1)* ~~(2 Pet. iii. 18; 1 Thess. iv. 1.)~~

Sanctification, again, is a thing which depends greatly on a diligent use of Scriptural means. When I speak of "means," I have in view

- Bible-reading,

- private prayer,

- regular attendance on public worship,

- regular hearing of God's Word,

- and regular reception of the Lord's
  Supper.

I lay it down as a simple matter of fact, that no one who is careless about such things must ever expect to make much progress in sanctification. I can find no record of any eminent saint who ever neglected them.

They are appointed channels through which the Holy Spirit conveys fresh supplies of grace to the soul, and strengthens the work which He has begun in the inward humans ~~man~~. Let people ~~men~~ call this legal doctrine if they please, but I will never shrink from declaring my belief that **there are no "spiritual gains without pains."**

> *I should as soon expect a farmer to prosper in business who contented* themself ~~himself~~ *with sowing* their ~~his~~ *fields and never looking at them*

till harvest, *as expect a believer to attain much holiness who was not diligent about his <u>Bible-reading, his prayers, and the use of his Sundays</u>.*

Our God is a God who works by means, and He will <u>never</u> bless the soul of that person ~~man~~ who pretends to be so high and spiritual that they ~~he~~ can get on without them.

Sanctification, again, is a thing which does not prevent a person ~~man~~ having a great deal of inward spiritual conflict. By conflict I mean a struggle within the heart between the old nature and the new, the flesh and the spirit, which are to be found together in every believer. *(Galatians 5:17)* ~~(Gal. v. 17.)~~

> **A deep sense of that struggle, and a vast amount of mental discomfort from it, are no proof that a person ~~man~~ is not sanctified. Nay, rather, I believe they are healthy symptoms of our condition, and prove that we are not dead, but alive, A true Christian is one who has not only peace of conscience, but war within.**

They ~~He~~ may be known by their ~~his~~ warfare as well as by their ~~his~~ peace. In saying this, I do not forget that I am contradicting the views of some well- meaning Christians, who hold the doctrine called "sinless perfection." I cannot help that. I believe that what I say is confirmed by the language of St. Paul in the seventh chapter of Romans. That chapter I commend to the careful study of all my readers. I am quite satisfied that it does not describe the experience of an unconverted person ~~man~~, or of a young and unestablished Christian; but of an old experienced saint in close communion with God. None but such a man could say,

"I delight in the law of God after the inward man." *(Romans 5:7)* ~~(Rom. vii. 22.)~~

I believe, furthermore, that what I say is proved by the experience of all the most eminent servants of Christ that have ever lived. The full proof is to be seen in their journals, their autobiographies, and their lives.

Believing all this, I shall never hesitate to tell people that inward conflict is no proof that a person ~~man~~ is not holy, and that they must not think they are not sanctified because they do not feel entirely free from inward struggle. Such freedom we shall doubtless have in heaven; but we shall never enjoy it in this world.

The heart of the best Christian, even at their ~~his~~ best, is a field occupied by two rival camps, and the "**company of two armies**." *(Song of Solomon 6:13)* ~~(Cant. vi. 13.)~~

Let the words of the Thirteenth and Fifteenth Articles be well considered by all Churchmen: "**The infection of nature doth remain in them that are regenerated.**" "**Although baptized and born again in Christ, we offend in many things; and if we say that we have no sin, we deceive ourselves, and the truth is not in us.**"

Sanctification, again, is a thing which cannot justify a human ~~man~~, and yet it pleases God.

This may seem wonderful, and yet it is true. The holiest actions of the holiest saint that ever lived are all more or less full of defects and imperfections. They are either wrong in their motive or defective in their performance, and in  themselves are nothing better than "splendid sins," deserving God's wrath and condemnation. To suppose that such actions can stand the severity of God's judgment, atone for sin, and merit heaven, is simply absurd. "**By the deeds of the law shall no flesh be justified.**" - "**We conclude that a man is justified by faith without the deeds of the law.**" *(Romans 5:7)* ~~(Rom. iii. 20-28.)~~

The only righteousness in which we can appear before God is the righteousness of another

- even the perfect righteousness of our Substitute and Representative, Jesus Christ the Lord. His work, and not our work, is our only title to heaven. This is a truth which we should be ready to die to maintain.

- For all this, however, the Bible distinctly teaches that the holy actions of a sanctified person ~~man~~, although imperfect, are pleasing in the sight of God.

  - "**With such sacrifices God is well pleased.**" *(Hebrews 13:16)* ~~(Heb. xiii. 16.)~~

- **"Obey your parents, for this is well pleasing to the Lord."** *(Colossians 3:20)* ~~(Col. iii. 20.)~~
- **"We do those things that are pleasing in His sight."** *(1 John 3:22)* ~~(1 John iii. 22.)~~

Let this never be forgotten, for it is a very comfortable doctrine. Just as a parent is pleased with the efforts of his little child to please them ~~him~~, though it be only by picking a daisy or walking across a room, so is our Father in heaven pleased with the poor performances of His believing children. He looks at the motive, principle, and intention of their actions, and not merely at their quantity and quality. He regards them as members of His own dear Son, and for His sake, wherever there is a single eye, He is well-pleased. Those Churchmen who dispute this would do well to study the Twelfth Article of the Church of England.

Sanctification, again, is a thing which will be found absolutely necessary as a witness to our character in the great day of judgment.

It will be utterly useless to plead that we believed in Christ, unless our faith has had some sanctifying effect, and been seen in our lives.

<u>Evidence, evidence, evidence,</u> will be the one thing wanted when the great white throne is set, when the books are opened, when the graves give up their tenants, when the dead are arraigned before the bar of God. Without some evidence that our faith in Christ was real and genuine, we shall only rise again to be condemned. I can find no evidence that will be admitted In that day, except sanctification.

The question will not be how we talked and what we professed, <u>but how we lived and what we did</u>. Let no man deceive himself on this point.

If anything is certain about the future, it is certain that there will be a judgment; and if anything is certain about judgment, it is certain that men's "works" and "doings" will be considered and examined in it. *(John 5:29) (2 Corinthians 5:10) (Revelation 20:13)* (John v. 29; 2 Cor. v. 10; Rev. xx. 13.)

They He that supposes works are of no importance, because they cannot justify us, <u>is a very ignorant Christian</u>. Unless they he opens their his eyes, they he will find to their his cost that if they come he comes to the bar of God without some evidence of grace, they he had better never have been born.

Sanctification, in the last place, is absolutely necessary in order to train and prepare us for heaven.

Most people men hope to go to heaven when they die; but few, it may be feared, take the trouble to consider whether they would enjoy heaven if they got there.

Heaven is essentially a holy place; its inhabitants are all holy; its occupations are all holy. To be really happy in heaven, it is clear and plain that we must be somewhat trained and made ready for heaven while we are on earth.

The notion of a purgatory after death, which shall turn sinners into saints, is a lying invention of humans man, and is nowhere taught in the Bible. We must be saints before we die, if we are to be saints afterwards in glory.

The favorite favourite idea of many, that dying people men need nothing except absolution and forgiveness of sins to fit them for their great change, is a profound delusion.

- We need the work of the Holy Spirit as well as the work of Christ;

- we need renewal of the heart as well as the atoning blood;

- we need to be sanctified as well as to be justified.

It is common to hear people <u>saying on their death-beds, "I only want the Lord to forgive me my sins, and take me to rest."</u> But those who say such things forget that the rest of heaven would be utterly useless if we had no heart to enjoy it!

What could an unsanctified person ~~man~~ do in heaven, if by any chance they ~~he~~ got there? Let that question be fairly looked in the face, and fairly answered. No person ~~man~~ can possibly be happy in a place where they are ~~he is~~ not in their ~~his~~ element, and where all around them ~~him~~ is not pleasant ~~congenial~~ to their ~~his~~ tastes, habits, and character. When an eagle is happy in an iron cage, when a sheep is happy in the water, when an owl is happy in the blaze of noonday sun, when a fish is happy on the dry land - **then, and not till then, will I admit that the unsanctified person ~~man~~ could be happy in heaven.**

I lay down these twelve propositions about sanctification with a firm persuasion that they are true, and I ask all who read these pages to ponder them well. Each of them would admit of being expanded and handled more fully, and all of them deserve private thought and consideration. Some of them may be disputed and contradicted; but I doubt whether any of them can be overthrown or proved untrue. I only ask for them a fair and impartial hearing. I believe in my conscience that they are likely to assist people ~~men~~ in attaining clear views of sanctification.

I now proceed to take up the second point which I proposed to consider. That point is the visible evidence of sanctification. In a word, what are the visible marks of a sanctified person ~~man~~? What may we expect to see in them ~~him~~?

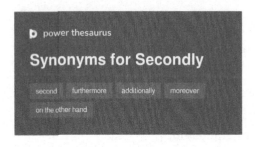

This is a very wide and difficult department of our subject. It is wide, because it necessitates the mention of many details which cannot be handled fully in the limits of a paper like this. It is difficult, because it cannot possibly be treated without giving offense ~~offence~~. But at any risk truth ought to be spoken; and there is some kind of truth which especially requires to be spoken in the present day.

True sanctification then does not consist in talk about religion.

This is a point which ought never to be forgotten. The vast increase of education and preaching in these latter days makes it absolutely necessary to raise a warning voice. <u>People hear so much of Gospel truth that they contract an unholy familiarity with its words and phrases, and sometimes talk so fluently about its doctrines that you might think them true Christians.</u>

In fact it is sickening and disgusting to hear the cool and flippant language which many pour out about "conversion

- the Savior ~~Saviour~~

- the Gospel

- finding peace

- free grace,"

and the like, while they are notoriously serving sin or living for the world.

Can we doubt that such talk is abominable in God's sight, and is little better than cursing, swearing, and taking God's name in vain?

The tongue is not the only member that Christ bids us give to His service. God does not want His people to be mere empty tubs, sounding brass and tinkling cymbals. We must be sanctified, not only **"in word and in tongue, but in deed and truth."** *(1 John 3:18)* ~~(1 John iii. 18.)~~

True sanctification does not consist in temporary religious feelings.

This again is a point about which a warning is greatly needed. Mission services and revival meetings are attracting great attention in every part of the land, and producing a great sensation. The Church of England seems to have taken a new lease of life, and exhibits a new activity; and we ought to thank God for it. But these things have their attendant dangers as well as their advantages. <u>Wherever wheat is sown the devil is sure to sow tares.</u> Many, it may be feared, appear moved and touched and roused under the preaching of the Gospel, while in reality their hearts are not changed at all.

A kind of animal excitement from the contagion of seeing others weeping, rejoicing, or affected, is the true account of their case. Their wounds are only skin deep, and the peace they profess to feel is skin deep also. Like the stony-ground hearers, they "receive the Word with joy" *(Matthew 13:20)* (Matt. xiii. 20); but after a little they fall away, go back to the world, and are harder and worse than before. Like Jonah's gourd, they come up suddenly in a night and perish in a night. Let these things not be forgotten.

Let us beware in this day of healing wounds slightly, and crying, Peace, peace, when there is no peace.

Let us urge on every one who exhibits new interest in religion to be content with nothing short of the deep, solid, sanctifying work of the Holy Ghost. <u>Reaction, after false religious excitement, is a most deadly disease of soul.</u> When the devil is only temporarily cast out of a man in the heat of a revival, and by and by returns to his house, the last state becomes worse than the first. Better a thousand times begin more slowly, and then "continue in the word" steadfastly, than begin in a hurry, without counting 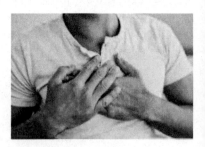 the cost, and by and by look back, with Lot's wife, and return to the world.

I declare I know no state of soul more dangerous than to imagine we are born again and sanctified by the Holy Ghost, because we have picked up a few religious feelings.

True sanctification does not consist in outward formalism and external devoutness. This is an enormous delusion, but unhappily a very common one. <u>Thousands appear to imagine that true holiness is to be seen in an excessive quantity of bodily religion</u>

- in constant attendance on Church services,

- reception of the Lord's Supper,

- and observance of fasts and saints' days

- in multiplied bowings and turnings and gestures and postures during public worship

- in self-imposed austerities and petty self- denials

- in wearing peculiar dresses, and the use of pictures and crosses.

I freely admit that some people take up these things from conscientious motives, and actually believe that they help their souls. But I am afraid that in many cases <u>this external religiousness is made a substitute for inward holiness</u>; and I am quite certain that it falls utterly short of sanctification of heart.

Above all, when I see that many followers of this outward, sensuous, and formal style of Christianity are absorbed in worldliness, and plunge headlong into its pomps and vanities, without shame, I feel that there is need of very plain speaking on the subject.

There may be an immense amount of "bodily service," while there is not a jot of real sanctification.

Sanctification does not consist in retirement from our place in life, and the renunciation of our social duties. In every age this has been a snare with many to take up this line in the pursuit of holiness. Hundreds of hermits have buried themselves in some wilderness, and thousands of men and women have shut themselves up within the walls of monasteries and convents, under the vain idea that by so doing they would escape sin and become eminently holy. They have forgotten that no bolts and bars can keep out the devil, and that, wherever we go, we carry that root of all evil, our own hearts.

To become a monk, or a nun, or to join a House of of Mercy, is not the high road to sanctification. True holiness does not make a Christian evade difficulties, but face and overcome them.

Christ would have His people show that His grace is not a mere hot -house plant, which can only thrive under shel-

ter, but a strong, hardy thing which can flourish in every relation of life.

It is doing our duty in that state to which God has called us

- like salt in the midst of corruption,

- and light in the midst of darkness

- which is a primary element in sanctification.

It is not the person ~~man~~ who hides themself ~~himself~~ in a cave, but the person ~~man~~ who glorifies God as master or servant, parent or child, in the family and in the street, in business and in trade, who is the Scriptural type of a sanctified person ~~man~~. Our Master Himself said in His last prayer, **"I pray not that Thou shouldest take them out of the world, but that Thou shouldest keep them from the evil."** *(John 17:15)* ~~(John xvii. 15.)~~

Sanctification does not consist in the occasional performance of right actions. It is the habitual working of a new heavenly principle within, which runs through all a

man's daily conduct, both in great things and in small.

Its seat is in the heart, and like the heart in the body, it has a regular influence on every part of the character. It is not like a pump, which only sends forth water when worked upon from without, but like a perpetual fountain, from which a stream is ever flowing spontaneously and naturally. Even Herod, when he heard John the Baptist, **"did many things,"** while his heart was utterly wrong in the sight of God. *(Mark 6:15)* ~~(Mark vi. 20.)~~

Just so there are scores of people in the present day who seem to have involuntary ~~spasmodical~~ fits of "goodness," as it is called, and do many right things under the influence of sickness, affliction, death in the family, public calamities, or a sudden qualm of conscience. Yet all the time any intelligent observer can see plainly that they are not converted, and that they know nothing of "sanctification." A true saint, like Hezekiah, will be whole-hearted. They He will **"count God's commandments concerning all things to be right, and hate every false way.**" *(2 Corinthians 1:21)* *(Psalms 119:104)* ~~(2 Chron. i. 21; Psalm cxix. 104.)~~

Genuine sanctification will show itself in habitual respect to God's law, and habitual effort to live in obedience to it as the rule of life.

There is no greater mistake than to suppose that a Christian has nothing to do with the law and the Ten Commandments, because they he cannot be justified by keeping them.

The same Holy Ghost who convinces the believer of sin by the law, and leads them him to Christ for justification, will always lead them him to a spiritual use of the law, as a friendly guide, in the pursuit of sanctification.

Our Lord Jesus Christ never made light of the Ten Commandments; on the contrary, in His first public discourse, the Sermon on the Mount, He expounded them, and showed the searching nature of their requirements.

- St. Paul never made light of the law: on the contrary, he says, "**The law is good, if a man use it lawfully.**" *(1 Timothy 1:8)* ~~(1 Tim. i. 8;~~
- "**I delight in the law of God after the inward man**", *(Romans 7:22)* ~~Rom. vii. 22.)~~

They He that pretends to be a saint, while they he sneers at the Ten Commandments, and thinks nothing of lying, hypocrisy, swindling, ill-temper, slander, drunkenness, and breach of the seventh commandment, **is under a fearful delusion**. They He will find it hard to prove that they are he is a "saint" in the last day!

Genuine sanctification will show itself in an habitual attempt ~~en-deavour~~ to do Christ's will, and to live by His practical precepts. These precepts are to be found scattered everywhere throughout the four Gospels, and especially in the Sermon on the Mount. They ~~He~~ that supposes they were spoken without the intention of promoting holiness, and that a Christian need not attend to them in their ~~his~~ daily life, is **really little better than a lunatic, and at any rate is a grossly ignorant person.**

To hear some people ~~men~~ talk, and read some others ~~men's~~ writings, one might imagine that our blessed Lord, when He was on earth, never taught anything but doctrine, and left practical duties to be taught by others! The slightest knowledge of the four Gospels ought to tell us that this is a complete mistake. What His disciples ought to be and to do is continually brought forward in our Lord's teaching. A truly sanctified person ~~man~~ will never forget this. They serve ~~He serves~~ a Master who said, **"You are my friends if you do whatever I command you."** *(John 15:14)* **~~"Ye are my friends if ye do whatsoever I command you." (John xv. 14.)~~**

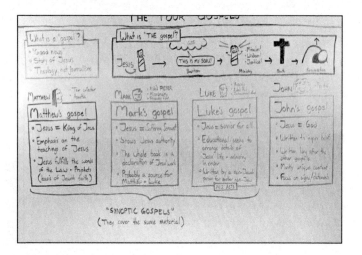

Genuine sanctification will show itself in an habitual desire to live up to the standard which St. Paul sets before the Churches in his writings. That standard is to be found in the closing chapters of nearly all his Epistles. The common idea of many persons that St. Paul's writings are full of nothing but doctrinal statements and controversial subjects

- justification,
- election,
- predestination,
- prophecy,

and the like is an entire delusion, and a melancholy proof of the ignorance of Scripture which prevails in these latter days.

I defy anyone to read St. Paul's writings carefully without finding in them a large quantity of plain, practical directions about the Christian's duty in every relation of life, and about our daily habits, temper, and behavior ~~behaviour~~ to one another. These directions were written down by inspiration of God for the perpetual guidance of professing Christians.

***They* ~~He~~ *who does not attend to them may possibly pass muster as a member of a church or a chapel, but* they ~~he~~ *certainly is not what the Bible calls a "sanctified"* per-son ~~man~~.**

Genuine sanctification will show itself in habitual attention to the active graces which our Lord so beautifully exemplified, and especially to the grace of charity.

> *"A new commandment I give unto you, that ye love one another; as I have loved you, that ye also love one another. By this shall all men know that ye are my disciples, if ye have love one to another." (John 13:34-35)* ~~(John xiii. 34, 35.)~~

A sanctified person ~~man~~ will try to do good in the world, and to lessen the sorrow and increase the happiness of all around them ~~him~~. They ~~He~~ will aim to be like his Master, full of kindness and love to every one; and this not in word only, by calling people "dear," but by deeds and actions and self-denying work, according as they have ~~he has~~ opportunity.

The selfish Christian professor, who wraps themself ~~himself~~ up in their ~~his~~ own conceit of superior knowledge, and seems to care nothing whether others sink or swim, go to heaven or hell, so long as they ~~he~~ walks to church or chapel in his Sunday best,

and is called a "sound member" - such a person ~~man~~ knows nothing of sanctification. They ~~He~~ may think himself a saint on earth, but they ~~he~~ will not be a saint in heaven. Christ will never be found the Savior ~~Saviour~~ of those who know nothing of following His example. Saving faith and real converting grace will always produce some conformity to the image of Jesus. (Colossians 3:10) ~~(Coloss. iii. 10.)~~

Genuine sanctification, in the last place, will show itself in habitual attention to the passive graces of Christianity. When I speak of

passive graces, I mean those graces which are especially shown in submission to the will of God, and in bearing and for bearing towards one another.

Few people, perhaps, unless they have examined the point, have an idea how much is said about these graces in the New Testament, and how important a place they seem to fill. This is the special point which St. Peter dwells upon in commending our Lord Jesus Christ's example to our notice:

"Christ also suffered for us, leaving us an example, that we should follow His steps: Who did no sin, neither was guile found in His mouth: Who, when He was reviled, reviled not again; when He suffered, He threatened not; but committed Himself to Him that judgeth righteously." (1 Peter 3:21-23) ~~(1 Peter ii. 21-23.)~~

- This is the one piece of profession which the Lord's prayer requires us to make: **"Forgive us our trespasses, as we forgive**

them that trespass against us"; and the one point that is commented upon at the end of the prayer.

This is the point which occupies one third of the list of the fruits of the Spirit, supplied by St. Paul. Nine are named, and three of these, "<u>long- suffering, gentleness, and meekness</u>," are unquestionably passive graces. (Galatians 5:22-23) ~~(Gal. v. 22, 23.)~~

I must plainly say that I do not think this subject is sufficiently considered by Christians. The passive graces are no doubt harder to attain than the active ones, but they are precisely the graces which have the greatest influence on the world. Of one thing I feel very sure

- it is nonsense to pretend to sanctification unless we follow after the meekness, gentleness, long-suffering, and forgiveness of which the Bible makes so much.

People who are habitually giving way to be easily irritated ~~peevish~~ and fast ~~cross~~ tempers in daily life, and are constantly sharp with their tongues, and disagreeable to all around them

- spiteful people,
- vindictive people,
- revengeful people,
- malicious people

of whom, alas, the world is only too full! all such know little, as they should know, about sanctification.

Such are the visible marks of a sanctified person ~~man~~. I do not say that they are all to be seen equally in all God's people. I freely admit that in the best they are not fully and perfectly exhibited. But I do say confidently, that the things of which I have been speaking are the Scriptural marks of sanctification, and that they who know nothing of them may well doubt whether they have any grace at all. Whatever others may please to say, I will never shrink from saying that genuine sanctification is a thing that can be seen, and that the marks I have attempted ~~endeavoured~~ to sketch out are more or less the marks of a sanctified person ~~man~~.

I now propose to consider, in the last place, the distinction between justification and sanctification.

Wherein do they agree, and wherein do they differ? This branch of our subject is one of great importance, though I fear it will not seem so to all my readers. I shall handle it briefly, but I dare not pass it over altogether.

Too many are apt to look at nothing but the surface of things in religion, and regard nice distinctions in theology as questions of "words and names," which are of little real value. But I warn all who are in earnest about their souls, that the discomfort which arises from not "distinguishing things that differ" in Christian doctrine is very great indeed; and I especially advise them, if they love peace, to seek clear views about the matter before us.

Justification and sanctification are two distinct things we must always remember. Yet there are points in which they agree and points in which they differ. Let us try to find out what they are.

In what, then, are justification and sanctification alike?

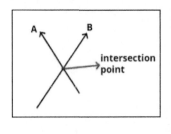

-Both proceed originally from the free grace of God. It is of His gift alone that believers are justified or sanctified at all.

-Both are part of that great work of salvation which Christ, in the eternal covenant, has undertaken on behalf of His people. Christ is the fountain of life, from which pardon and holiness both flow. The root of each is Christ.

- Both are to be found in the same persons. Those who are justified are always sanctified, and those who are sanctified are always justified. God has joined them together, and they cannot be put asunder.

- Both begin at the same time. The moment a person begins to be a justified person, they ~~he~~ also begins to be a sanctified person. They ~~He~~ may not feel it, but it is a fact.

- Both are alike necessary to salvation. No one ever reached heaven without a renewed heart as well as forgiveness, without the Spirit's grace as well as the blood of Christ, without a suitableness ~~meetness~~ for eternal glory as well as a title. The one is just as necessary as the other.

Such are the points on which justification and sanctification agree.

Let us now reverse the picture, and see wherein they differ.

- Justification is the reckoning and counting a person ~~man~~ to be righteous for the sake of another, even Jesus Christ the Lord. Sanctification is the actual making a person ~~man~~ inwardly righteous, though it may be in a very feeble degree.

- The righteousness we have by our justification is not our own, but the everlasting perfect righteousness of our great Mediator Christ, imputed to us, and made our own by faith.

- The righteousness we have by sanctification is our own righteousness, imparted, inherent, and wrought in us by the Holy Spirit, but mingled with much infirmity and imperfection.

- In justification our own works have no place at all, and simple faith in Christ is the one thing needful. In sanctification our own works are of vast importance and God bids us fight, and watch, and pray, and strive, and take pains, and labour.

- Justification is a finished and complete work, and a person ~~man~~ is perfectly justified the moment they believe ~~he believes~~. Sanctification is an imperfect work, comparatively, and will never be perfected until we reach heaven.

- Justification admits of no growth or increase: a person ~~man~~ is as much justified the hour they ~~he~~ first comes to Christ by faith as he will be to all eternity. Sanctification is eminently a progressive work, and admits of continual growth and enlargement so long as a person ~~man~~ lives.

- Justification has special reference to our persons, our standing in God's sight, and our deliverance from guilt. Sanctification has special reference to our natures, and the moral renewal of our hearts.

- Justification gives us our title to heaven, and boldness to enter in. Sanctification gives us our meetness for heaven, and prepares us to enjoy it when we dwell there.

- Justification is the act of God about us, and is not easily discerned by others. Sanctification is the work of God within us, and cannot be hid in its outward manifestation from the eyes of men.

I commend these distinctions to the attention of all my readers, and I ask them to ponder them well. I am persuaded that one great cause of the darkness and uncomfortable feelings of many well-meaning people in the matter of religion, is their habit of confounding, and not distinguishing, justification and sanctification.

It can never be too strongly impressed on our minds that they are two separate things. No doubt they cannot be divided, and everyone that is a partaker of either is a partaker of both. But never, never ought they to be confounded, and never ought the distinction between them to be forgotten.

It only remains for me now to bring this subject to a conclusion by a few plain words of application. The nature and visible marks of sanctification have been brought before us.

What practical reflections ought the whole matter to raise in our minds?

For one thing, let us all awake to a sense of the perilous state of many professing Christians. "Without holiness no man shall see the Lord"; without sanctification there is no salvation. (Hebrews 12:14) ~~(Heb. xii. 14.)~~

Then what an enormous amount of so-called religion there is which is perfectly <u>useless</u>!

What an immense proportion of church-goers and chapel-goers are in the broad road that leads ~~leadeth~~ to destruction!

The thought is awful, crushing, and overwhelming. Oh, that preachers and teachers would open their eyes and realize the condition of souls around them!

Oh, that people ~~men~~ could be persuaded to "**flee from the wrath to come** "! If unsanctified souls can be saved and go to heaven, <u>the Bible is not true</u>. <u>Yet the Bible is true and cannot lie!</u> What must the end be!

For another thing, let us make sure work of our own condition, and never rest till we feel and know that we are "sanctified" ourselves.

What are our tastes, and choices, and likings, and inclinations? This is the great testing question. It matters little what we wish, and what we hope, and what we desire to be before we die.

Where are we now?

What are we doing?

Are we sanctified or not? If not, the fault is all our own.

For another thing, if we would be sanctified, our course is clear and plain - we must begin with Christ. We must go to Him as sinners, with no plea but that of utter need, and cast our souls on

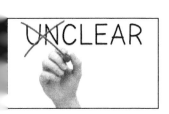

Him by faith, for peace and reconciliation with God. We must place ourselves in His hands, as in the hands of a good physician, and cry to Him for mercy and grace. We must wait for nothing to bring with us as a recommendation.

The very first step towards sanctification, no less than justification, is to <u>come with faith to Christ</u>. We must first live and then work.

For another thing, if we would grow in holiness and become more sanctified, we must continually go on as we began, and be ever making fresh applications to Christ.

He is the Head from which every member must be supplied. (Ephesians 4:16) ~~(Ephes. iv. 16.)~~ To live the life of daily faith in the Son of God, and to be daily drawing out of His fulness the promised grace and strength which He has laid up for His people - this is the grand secret of progressive sanctification.

Believers who seem at a standstill are generally neglecting close communion with Jesus, and so grieving the Spirit.

He that prayed, "Sanctify them," the last night before His crucifixion, is infinitely willing to help everyone who by faith applies to Him for help, and desires to be made more holy.

For another thing, let us not expect too much from our own hearts here below. At our best we shall find in ourselves daily cause for humiliation, and discover that we are needy debtors to mercy and grace every hour. The more light we have, the more we shall see our own imperfection. Sinners we were when we began, sinners we shall find ourselves as we go on; renewed, pardoned, justified - yet sinners to the very last. Our absolute perfection is yet to come, and the expectation of it is one reason why we should long for heaven.

Finally, let us never be ashamed of making much of sanctification, and contending for a high standard of holiness. While some are satisfied with a miserably low degree of attainment, and others are not ashamed to live on without any holiness at all

- content with a mere round of church

- going and chapel

- going, but never getting on, like a horse in a mill

let us stand fast in the old paths, follow after eminent holiness ourselves, and recommend it boldly to others. This is the only way to be really happy.

Let us feel convinced, whatever others may say, that holiness is happiness, and that the humans ~~man~~ who gets through life most comfortably is the sanctified person ~~man~~.

No doubt there are some true Christians who from ill - health, or family trials, or other secret causes, enjoy little sensible comfort, and go mourning all their days on the way to heaven. But these are exceptional cases.

As a general rule, in the long run of life, it will be found true that "sanctified" people are the happiest people on earth.

They have solid comforts which the world can neither give nor take away.

- "The ways of wisdom are ways of pleasantness." (Proverbs 3:17) (Prov iii. 17;

- "Great peace have they that love Thy law." (Psalms 119:165) Ps. cxix. 165;

- It was said by One who cannot lie, "My yoke is easy, and my burden is light." (Matthew 11:30) Matt. xi. 30

- But it is also written, "There is no peace unto the wicked."; (Isaiah 48:22) Is. xlviii. 22.)

P. S. The subject of sanctification is of such deep importance, and the mistakes made about it so many and great, that I make no apology for strongly recommending "Owen on the Holy Spirit" to all who want to study more thoroughly the whole doctrine of sanctification. No single paper like this can embrace it all.

I am quite aware that Owen's writings are not fashionable in the present day, and that many think fit to neglect and sneer at him as a Puritan! Yet the great divine who in Commonwealth times was Dean of Christ Church, Oxford, does not deserve to be treated in this way. He had more learning and sound knowledge of Scripture in his little finger than many who depreciate him have in their whole bodies. I assert unhesitatingly that the person man who wants to study experimental theology will find no books equal to those of Owen and some of his contemporaries, for complete, Scriptural, and exhaustive treatment of the subjects they handle.

There is mention in the Scripture of a twofold sanctification, and consequently in a twofold holiness. The first is common unto persons and things, consisting of the peculiar dedication, consecration, or separation of them unto the service of God, by His own appointment, whereby they become holy. Thus the priests and Levites of old, the ark, the altar, the tabernacle, and the temple, were sanctified and made holy; and, indeed, in all holiness whatever, there is a peculiar dedication and separation unto God. But in the sense mentioned, this was solitary and alone. No more belonged unto it but this sacred separation, nor was there any other effect of this sanctification.

But, secondly, there is another kind of sanctification and holiness, wherein this separation to God is not the first thing done or intended, but a consequent and effect thereof. This is real and internal, by the communicating of a principle of holiness unto our natures, attended with its exercise in acts and duties of holy obedience unto God. This is that which we inquire after." - John Owen on the Holy Spirit. Vol. iii, p. 370, Works, Goold's edition.

<u>"The devil's war is better than the devil's peace. Suspect dumb holiness. When the dog is kept out of doors he howls to be let in again."</u> - "Contraries meeting, such as fire and water, conflict one with another. - When Satan finds ~~findeth~~ a sanctified heart, he tempts ~~tempteth~~ with much importunity. Where there is much of God and of Christ, there are strong injections and firebrands cast in at the windows, so that some of much faith have been tempted to doubt." - Rutherford's Trial of Faith, p. 403.

"There is no imagination wherewith a person ~~man~~ is besotted, more foolish, none so pernicious, as this, - that persons not purified, not sanctified, not made holy in their life, should afterwards be taken into that state of blessedness which consists in the enjoyment of God.<u> Neither can such persons enjoy God, nor would God be a reward to them</u>. - Holiness indeed is perfected in heaven: but the beginning of it is invariably confined to this world." - Owen on Holy Spirit, p. 575. Goold's edition.

"Christ in the Gospel is proposed to us as our pattern and example of holiness; and as it is a cursed imagination that this was the whole end of his life and death: namely, to exemplify and confirm the doctrine of holiness which He taught - so to neglect His being our example, in considering Him by faith to that end, and labouring after conformity to Him, is evil and pernicious. Wherefore let us be much in the contemplation of what He was, and what He did, and how in all duties and trials He carried Himself, until an image or idea of His perfect holiness is implanted in our minds, and we are made like unto Him thereby." - Owen on the Holy Ghost, p. 513. Goold's edition.

3 - HOLINESS

"Holiness, without which no man shall see the Lord."

Hebrews 12:14

The text which heads this page opens up a subject of deep importance. That subject is practical holiness. It suggests a question which demands the attention of all professing Christians

- Are we holy?

- Shall we see the Lord?

That question can never be out of season. The wise man tells us, **"There is a time to weep, and a time to laugh - a time to keep silence, and a time to speak"** (Ecclesiastes 3:4) ~~(Eccles. iii. 4, 7)~~; but there is no time, no, not a day, in which a man ought not to be holy.

Are we? That question concerns all ranks and conditions of humans ~~men~~.

- Some are rich and some are poor

- some learned and some unlearned

- some masters, and some servants; (MMLJ Publishers comment inserted - Slavery still Exists in 2022 - www.ilo.org - Fifty million people were living in modern slavery in 2021, according to the latest Global Estimates of Modern Slavery. Of these people, 28 million were in forced labour and 22 million were trapped in forced marriage. The number of people in modern slavery has risen significantly in the last five years. 10 million more people were in modern slavery in 2021 compared to 2016 global estimates. Women and children remain disproportionately vulnerable.)

- but there is no rank or condition in life in which a man ought not to be holy. Are we?

I ask to be heard today about this question.

How stands the account between our souls and God?

In this hurrying, bustling world, let us stand still for a few minutes and consider the matter of holiness. I believe I might have chosen a subject more popular and pleasant. I am sure I might have found one more easy to handle. But I feel deeply I could not have chosen one more seasonable and more profitable to our souls. It is an awakening thing to hear the Word of God saying,

"Without holiness no man shall see the Lord." *(Hebrews 12:14)* (Heb. xii. 14.)

I shall endeavor endeavour, by God's help, to examine what true holiness is, and the reason why it is so needful.

In conclusion, I shall try to point out the only way in which holiness can be attained. I have already, in the second paper in this volume, approached this subject from a doctrinal side. Let me now try to present it to my readers in a more plain and practical point of view.

First, then, let me try to show what true practical holiness is - what sort of persons are those whom God calls holy.

A human man may go great lengths, and yet never reach true holiness. It is not knowledge

- Balaam had that: nor great profession

- Judas Iscariot had that: nor doing many things
- Herod had that: nor zeal for certain matters in religion
- Jehu had that: nor morality and outward respectability of conduct - the young ruler had that: nor taking pleasure in hearing preachers
- the Jews in Ezekiel's time had that: nor keeping company with godly people
- Joab and Gehazi and Demas had that.

Yet none of these was holy! These things alone are not holiness. A human ~~man~~ may have any one of them, and yet never see the Lord.

What then is true practical holiness?

It is a hard question to answer. I do not mean that there is any want of Scriptural matter on the subject. But I fear lest I should give a defective view of holiness, and not say all that ought to be said; or at least ~~lest~~ I should say things about it that ought not to be said, and so do harm. Let me, however, try to draw a picture of holiness, that we may see it clearly before the eyes of our minds. Only let it never be forgotten, when I have said all, that <u>my account is but a poor imperfect outline at the best.</u>

Holiness is the habit of being of one mind with God, according as we find His mind described in Scripture. It is the habit of agreeing in God's judgment

- hating what He hates
- loving what He loves
- and measuring everything in this world by the standard of His Word.

They ~~He~~ who most entirely agrees with God, they are ~~he is~~ the most holy person ~~man~~.

A holy person ~~man~~ will endeavor ~~endeavour~~ to shun every known sin, and to keep every known commandment. They ~~He~~ will have a decided bent of mind toward God, a hearty desire to do His will - **a greater fear of displeasing Him than of displeasing the world**, and a love to all His ways.

He will feel what Paul felt when he said,"**I delight in the law of God after the inward man**" *(Romans 7:22)* ~~(Rom. vii. 22)~~,

and what David felt when he said, "**I esteem all Thy precepts concerning all things to be right, and I hate every false way.**" *(Psalms 119:128)* ~~(Psalm cxix. 128.)~~

A holy person ~~man~~ will strive to be like our Lord Jesus Christ. They ~~He~~ will not only live the life of faith in Him, and draw from Him all his daily peace and strength, but he will also labour to have the mind that was in Him, and to be "**conformed to His image.**" *(Romans 8:29)* ~~(Rom. viii. 29.)~~

It will be their ~~his~~ aim to bear with and forgive others, even as Christ forgave us

- to be unselfish, even as Christ pleased not Himself

- to walk in love, even as Christ loved us -

- to be lowly-minded and humble, even as Christ made Himself of no reputation and humbled Himself. He will remember that Christ was a faithful witness for the truth

- that He came not to do His own will

- that it was His meat and drink to do His Father's will

- that He would continually deny Himself in order to minister to others

- that He was meek and patient under undeserved insults

- that He thought more of godly poor men than of kings

- that He was full of love and compassion to sinners

- that He was bold and uncompromising in denouncing sin

- that He sought not the praise of men, when He might have had it

- that He went about doing good

- that He was separate from worldly people

- that He continued instant in prayer

- that He would not let even His nearest relations stand in His way when God's work was to be done.

These things a holy person ~~man~~ will try to remember. By them they ~~he~~ will endeavour to shape their ~~his~~ course in life.

They ~~He~~ will lay to heart the saying of John, "**He that saith he abideth in Christ ought himself also so to walk, even as He walked**" *(1 John 2:6)* ~~(1 John ii. 6)~~;

and the saying of Peter, that "**Christ suffered for us, leaving us an example that ye should follow His steps.**" *(1 Peter 2:21)* ~~(1 Peter ii. 21.)~~

Happy is whom ~~he who~~ has learned to make Christ his "all," both for salvation and example!

Much time would be saved, and much sin prevented, if humans ~~men~~ would more often ~~oftener~~ ask themselves the question, "**What would Christ have said and done, if He were in my place?**"

A holy person ~~man~~ will follow after meekness, long-suffering, gentleness, patience, kind tempers, government of their ~~his~~ tongue. They ~~He~~ will bear much, forbear much, overlook much, and be slow to talk of standing on his rights. We see a bright example of this in the behavior ~~behaviour~~ of David when Shimei cursed him - and of Moses when Aaron and Miriam spake against him. *(2 Samual 16:10) (Number 12:3)* ~~(2 Sam. xvi. 10; Num. xii. 3.)~~

A holy person ~~man~~ will follow after temperance and self-denial. They ~~He~~ will labor ~~labour~~ to mortify the desires of his body

-to crucify their ~~his~~ flesh with his affections and lusts

-to curb their ~~his~~ passions

-to restrain their ~~his~~ carnal inclinations, lest at any time they break loose.

Oh, what a word is that of the Lord Jesus to the Apostles, "So be careful, or your hearts will be loaded down with carousing, drunkenness, and cares of this life, and that day will come on you suddenly. For it will come like a snare on all those who dwell on the surface of all the earth. Therefore be watchful all the time, praying that you may be counted worthy to escape all these things that will happen, and to stand before the Son of Man" *(Luke 21:34-36)*

~~"Take heed to yourselves, lest at any time your hearts be overcharged with surfeiting and drunkenness, and cares of this life" (Luke xxi. 34);~~

and that of the Apostle Paul, "Don't you know that those who run in a race all run, but one receives the prize? Run like that, so that you may win. Every man who strives in the games exercises self-control in all things. Now they do it to receive a corruptible crown, but we an incorruptible. I therefore run like that, not aimlessly. I fight like that, not beating the air, but I beat my body and bring it into submission, lest by any means, after I have preached to others, I myself should be disqualified." *(1 Corinthians 9:24-27)*

~~"I keep under my body, and bring it into subjection, lest that by any means when I have preached to others, I myself should be a castaway." (1 Cor. ix. 27.)~~

A holy person ~~man~~ will follow after charity and brotherly kindness. They ~~He~~ will endeavour to observe the <u>golden rule of doing as he would have men do to him</u>, and <u>speaking as he would have men speak to him</u>. They ~~He~~ will be full of affection towards his brethren towards their bodies, their property, their characters, their feelings, their souls. "**He that loveth another,**" says Paul, "**hath fulfilled the law.**" *(Romans 13:8)* ~~(Rom. xiii. 8.)~~

He will abhor all lying, slandering, backbiting, cheating, dishonesty, and unfair dealing, even in the least things. The shekel and cubit of the sanctuary were larger than those in common use. They ~~He~~ will strive to adorn their ~~his~~ religion by all his outward behavior ~~demeanour~~, and to make it lovely and beautiful in the eyes of all around him. Alas, what condemning words are the 13th chapter of 1 Corinthians, and the Sermon on the Mount, when laid alongside the conduct of many professing Christians!

A holy person ~~man~~ will follow after a spirit of mercy and benevolence towards others. They ~~He~~ will not stand all the day idle. They

He will not be content with doing no harm - they He will try to do good. They He will strive to be useful in his day and generation, and to lessen the spiritual wants and misery around him, as far as he can. Such was Dorcas, **"full of good works and charity almsdeeds, which she did,"** - not merely purposed and talked about, but did. Such an one was Paul: **"I will very gladly spend and be spent for you,"** he says, **"though the more abundantly I love you the less I be loved."** *(Acts 9:36) (2 Corinthians 12:15)* (Acts ix. 36; 2 Cor. xii. 15.)

- A holy person man will follow after purity of heart.

-They He will dread all filthiness and uncleanness of spirit, and seek to avoid all things that might draw him into it.

-They know He knows their his own heart is like tinder, and will diligently keep clear of the sparks of temptation.

Who shall dare to talk of strength when David can fall? There is many a hint to be gleaned from the ceremonial law. Under it the humans man who only touched a bone, or a dead body, or a grave, or a diseased person, became at once unclean in the sight of God. And these things were symbols emblems and figures. ***Few Christians are ever too watchful and too particular about this point.***

- holy person man will follow after the fear of God.
- I do not mean the fear of a slave, who only works because they are he is afraid of punishment, and would be idle if they he did not dread discovery.
- I mean rather the fear of a child, who wishes to live and move as if they have he was always before their his fathers face, because they love he loves him.

What a noble example Nehemiah gives us of this! When he became Governor at Jerusalem he might have been chargeable to the Jews and required of them money for his support. The former Governors had done so. There was none to blame him if he did. But he says, **"So did not I, because of the fear of God."** *(Nehemiah 5:15)* (Nehem. v. 15.)

- A holy person ~~man~~ will follow after humility.
- They ~~He~~ will desire, in lowliness of mind, to esteem all others better than himself.
- They ~~He~~ will see more evil in his own heart than in any other in the world.
- They ~~He~~ will understand something of Abraham's feeling, when he says, "**I am dust and ashes**;"
- and Jacob's, when he says, "**I am less than the least of all Thy mercies;**"
- and Job's, when he says, "**I am vile**;"

-and Paul's, when he says, "**I am chief of sinners.**"

-Holy Bradford, that faithful martyr of Christ, would sometimes finish his letters with these words, "A most miserable sinner, John Bradford."

-Good old Mr. Grimshaw's last words, when he lay on his death-bed, were these, "Here goes an unprofitable servant."

A holy person ~~man~~ will follow after faithfulness in all the duties and relations in life.

They ~~He~~ will try, not merely to fill his place as well as others who take no thought for their souls, but even better, because he has higher motives, and more help than they. Those words of Paul should never be forgotten,

- "Whatever ye do, do it heartily, as unto the Lord," *(Colossians 3:23)* ~~(Col. iii. 23;~~
- "Not slothful in business, fervent in spirit, serving the Lord." *(Romans 12:11)* ~~Rom. xii. 11.)~~

Holy persons should aim at doing everything well, and should be ashamed of allowing themselves to do anything ill if they can help it. Like Daniel, they should seek to give no "**occasion**" against themselves, except "**concerning the law of their God.**" *(Daniel 6:5)* ~~(Dan. vi. 5.)~~

They should strive to be good husbands and good wives, good parents and good children, good masters and good servants, good neighbors ~~neighbours~~, good friends, good subjects, good in private and good in public, good in the place of business and good by their firesides. <u>Holiness is worth little indeed, if it does not bear this kind of fruit.</u>

The Lord Jesus puts a searching question to His people, when He says, " If you only greet your friends, what more do you do than others? Don't even the tax collectors do the same?" *(Matthew 55:47)* ~~"What do ye more than others?" (Matt. v. 47.)~~

Last, but not least, a holy man will follow after spiritual mindedness.

They ~~He~~ will attempt ~~endeavour~~ to set his affections entirely on things above, and to hold things on earth with a very loose hand.

They ~~He~~ will not neglect the business of the life that now is; but the first place in his mind and thoughts will be given to the life to come.

They ~~He~~ will aim to live like one whose treasure is in heaven, and to pass through this world like a stranger and pilgrim traveling to his home.

To commune with God in prayer, in the Bible, and in the assembly of His people - these things will be the holy man's chiefest enjoyments.

EVERYTHING IS POSSIBLE FOR ONE WHO BELIEVES.

MARK 9:23

They ~~He~~ will value every thing and place and company, just in proportion as it draws him nearer to God.

They ~~He~~ will enter into something of David's feeling, when he says,

"My soul stays close to you. Your right hand holds me up" and "Yahweh is my portion. I promised to obey your words" *(Psalms 63:8 & 119:57)*

~~"My soul followeth hard after Thee." "Thou art my portion."(Psalm lxiii. 8; cxix. 57.)~~

Such is the outline of holiness which I venture to sketch out. Such is the character which those who are called "holy" follow after. Such are the main features of a holy person ~~man~~.

But here let me say, I trust no human ~~man~~ will misunderstand me. I am not without fear that my meaning will be mistaken, and the description I have given of holiness will discourage some tender conscience (feeling). I would not willingly make one righteous heart sad, or throw a stumbling-block in any believer's way.

I do not say for a moment that holiness shuts out the presence of indwelling sin. No: far from it. It is the greatest misery of a holy person ~~man~~ that they carry ~~he carries~~ about with themselves ~~him~~ a "body of death;"

- that often when he would do good "evil is present with him"; that the old man is clogging all his movements, and, as it were, trying to draw him back at every step he takes. "Don't be overcome by evil, but overcome evil with good." *(Romans 12:11)* ~~(Rom. vii. 21.)~~

But it is the excellence of a holy person ~~man~~ that they are ~~he is~~ not at peace with indwelling sin, as others are.

They ~~He~~ hates it, mourns over it, and longs to be free from its company.

The work of sanctification within him is like the wall of Jerusalem - the building goes forward "**even in troublous times.**" *(Daniel 9:25)* ~~(Dan. ix. 25.)~~

Neither do I say that holiness comes to ripeness and perfection all at once, or that these graces I have touched on must be found in full bloom and sturdiness ~~vigour~~ before you can call a person ~~man~~ holy. No: far from it.

Sanctification is always a progressive work.

Some peoples ~~men's~~ graces are in the blade, some in the ear, and some are like full corn in the ear. All must have a beginning. We must never despise "**the day of small things.**"

And sanctification in the very best is an imperfect work.

The history of the brightest saints that ever lived will contain many a "<u>but</u>," and "<u>howbeit</u>," and "<u>notwithstanding</u>," before you reach the end. The gold will never be without some dross - the light will never shine without some clouds, until we reach the heavenly Jerusalem. The sun himself has spots upon his face.

The holiest people ~~men~~ have many a blemish and defect when weighed in the balance of the sanctuary.

Their life is a continual warfare with sin, the world, and the devil; and sometimes you will see them not overcoming, but overcome.

"For the flesh lusts against the Spirit, and the Spirit against the flesh; and these are contrary to one another, that you may not do the things that you desire." *(Galatians 5:17)*

~~The flesh is ever lusting against the spirit, and the spirit against the flesh, (Gal. v. 17)~~

and **"For we all stumble in many things. Anyone who doesn't stumble in word is a perfect person, able to bridle the whole body also."** *(James 3:2)*

~~"in many things they offend all.";~~ ~~(James iii. 2.)~~

But still, for all this, I am sure that to have such a character as I have faintly drawn, is the heart's desire and prayer of all true Christians. They press towards it, if they do not reach it. They may not attain to it, but they always aim at it. It is what they strive and labor ~~labour~~ to be, if it is not what they are.

And this I do boldly and confidently say, that true holiness is a great reality.

- It is something in a person ~~man~~ that can be seen, and known, and marked, and felt by all around them ~~him~~.

- It is light: if it exists, it will show itself.
- It is salt: if it exists, its taste ~~savour~~ will be perceived. It is a precious ointment: if it exists, its presence cannot be hid.

I am sure we should all be ready to make allowance for much backsliding, for much occasional deadness in professing Christians. I know a road may lead from one point to another, and yet have many a winding and turn; and a person ~~man~~ may be truly holy, and yet be drawn aside by many an infirmity.

Gold is not the less gold because mingled with alloy, nor light the less light because faint and dim, nor grace the less grace because young and weak.

But after every allowance, I cannot see how any person ~~man~~ deserves to be called "holy," who intentionally ~~wilfully~~ allows themselves to sin ~~himself in sins,~~ and is not humbled and ashamed because of them.

I dare not call anyone "holy" who makes a habit of intentionally ~~wilfully~~ neglecting known duties, and intentionally ~~wilfully~~ doing what he knows God has commanded him not to do. Well says Owen, "I do not understand how a person ~~man~~ can be a true believer unto whom sin is not the greatest burden, sorrow, and trouble."

Such are the leading characteristics of practical holiness. Let us examine ourselves and see whether we are acquainted with it. Let us prove our own selves.

Let me try, in the next place, to show some reasons why practical holiness is so important.

Can holiness save us?

Can holiness put away sin

- cover iniquities
- make satisfaction for transgressions
- pay our debt to God?

No: not what so ever ~~a whit~~. God forbid that I should ever say so. Holiness can do none of these things.

The brightest saints are all "unprofitable servants." Our purest works are no better than filthy rags, when tried by the light of God's holy law. The white robe which Jesus offers, and faith puts on, must be our only righteousness

- *the name of Christ our only confidence*
- *the Lamb's book of life our only title to heaven.*
- *With all our holiness we are no better than sinners.*
- *Our best things are stained and tainted with imperfection.*

They are all more or less incomplete, wrong in the motive or defective in the performance. By the deeds of the law shall no child of Adam ever be justified.

"for by grace you have been saved through faith, and that not of yourselves; it is the gift of God, not of works, that no one would boast." *(Ephesians 2:8-9)*

~~"By grace are ye saved through faith, and that not of yourselves, it is the gift of God: not of works, lest any man should boast." (Ephes. ii. 8, 9.)~~

Why then is holiness so important?

Why does the Apostle say, **"Without it no man shall see the Lord"**? Let me set out in order a few reasons.

For one thing, we must be holy, because the voice of God in Scripture plainly commands it. The Lord Jesus says to His people,

"Except your righteousness shall exceed the righteousness of the scribes and Pharisees, ye shall in no case enter into the kingdom of heaven." *(Matthew 5:20)* ~~(Matt. v. 20.)~~

"Be ye perfect, even as your Father which is in heaven is perfect." *(Matthew 5:48)* ~~(Matt. v. 48.)~~

Paul tells the Thessalonians, **"This is the will of God, even your sanctification."** *(1 Thessalonians 4:3)* ~~(1 Thess. iv. 3.)~~

And Peter says, **"but just as he who called you is holy, you yourselves also be holy in all of your behavior, because it is written, "You shall be holy, for I am holy."** *(1 Peter 1:15-16)*
~~"As He which hath called you is holy, so be ye holy in all manner of conversation;" because it is written, "Be ye holy, for I am holy."(1 Peter i. 15, 16.)~~

"In this," says Leighton, "law and Gospel agree."

- We must be holy, because this is one grand end and purpose for which Christ came into the world.
- Paul writes to the Corinthians, **"He died for all, that they which live should not henceforth live unto themselves, but unto Him which died for them and rose again."** *(2 Corinthians 5:15)* ~~(2 Cor. v. 15.)~~
- And to the Ephesians, **"Christ loved the Church, and gave Himself for it, that He might sanctify and cleanse it."** *(Ephesians 5:25-26)* ~~(Ephes. v. 25, 26.)~~
- And to Titus, **"He gave Himself for us, that He might redeem us from all iniquity, and purify unto Himself a peculiar people, zealous of good works."** *(Titus 2:14)* ~~(Titus ii. 14.)~~

In short, to talk of people ~~men~~ being saved from the guilt of sin, without being at the same time saved from its dominion in their hearts, is to contradict the witness of all Scripture.

- Are believers said to be elect! it is "through sanctification of the Spirit." *(1 Peter 1:2)* ~~(1 Peter i. 2)~~

- Are they predestinated? - it is "to be conformed to the image of God's Son." *(Romans 8:29)* ~~(Rom. viii. 29)~~

- Are they chosen? - it is "that they may be holy." *(Ephesians 1:4)* ~~(Eph. i. 4)~~

- Are they called? - is it "with a holy calling." *(Hebrews 12:10)* ~~(Heb. xii. 10)~~

- Are they afflicted? - it is that they may be "partakers of holiness."

Jesus is a complete Savior ~~Saviour~~. He does not merely take away the guilt of a believer's sin, He does more - He breaks its power.

We must be holy, because this is the only sound evidence that we have a saving faith in our Lord Jesus Christ. The Twelfth Article of our Church says truly, that

"Although good works cannot put away our sins, and endure the severity of God's judgment, yet are they pleasing and acceptable to God in Christ, and do spring out necessarily of a true and lively faith; in so much that by them a lively faith may be as evidently known as a tree discerned by its fruits."

James warns us there is such a thing as a dead faith

- a faith which goes no further than the profession of the lips, and has no influence on a man's character. *(James 2:17)* ~~(James ii. 17.)~~

- True saving faith is a very different kind of thing. True faith will always show itself by its fruits

- it will sanctify, it will work by love, it will overcome the world, it will purify the heart.

I know that people are fond of talking about death-bed evidences. They will rest on words spoken in the hours of fear, and pain, and weakness, as if they might take comfort in them about the friends they lose. But I am afraid <u>in ninety-nine cases out of a hundred</u> such evidences are not to be depended on. I suspect that, with rare exceptions, men die just as they have lived.

The only safe evidence that we are one with Christ, and Christ in us, is holy life.

They that live unto the Lord are generally the only people who die in the Lord. If we would die the death of the righteous, let us not rest in slothful desires only; let us seek to live His life.

It is a true saying of Traill's, "That a humans ~~man's~~ state is nothing ~~naught~~, and their ~~his~~ faith unsound, that find not their ~~his~~ hopes of glory purifying to their ~~his~~ heart and life."

We must be holy, because this is the only proof that we love the Lord Jesus Christ in sincerity.

This is a point on which He has spoken most plainly, in the fourteenth and fifteenth chapters of John.

- "If ye love Me, keep my commandments." *(John 14:15)* ~~(John xiv. 15)~~
- "He that hath my commandments and keepeth them, he it is that loveth Me." *(John 14:21)* ~~(John xiv. 21)~~
- "If a man love Me he will keep my words." *(John 14:23)* ~~(John xiv. 23)~~
- "Ye are my friends if ye do whatsoever I command you." *(John 15:14)* ~~(John xv. 14.)~~

Plainer words than these it would be difficult to find, and woe to those who neglect them! Surely that humans ~~man~~ must be in an unhealthy state of soul who can think of all that Jesus suffered, and yet cling to those sins for which that suffering was undergone

- It was sin that wove the crown of thorns
- it was sin that pierced our Lord's hands, and feet, and side
- it was sin that brought Him to Gethsemane and Calvary, to the cross and to the grave.

Cold must our hearts be if we do not hate sin and labor ~~labour~~ **to get rid of it, though we may have to cut off the right hand and pluck out the right eye in doing it.**

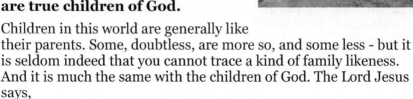

We must be holy, because this is the only sound evidence that we are true children of God.

Children in this world are generally like their parents. Some, doubtless, are more so, and some less - but it is seldom indeed that you cannot trace a kind of family likeness. And it is much the same with the children of God. The Lord Jesus says,

- **"If ye were Abraham's children ye would do the works of Abraham."** *(John 8:39)* ~~(John viii. 39)~~
- **"If God were your Father ye would love Me."** *(John 8:42)* ~~(John viii. 39, 42.)~~
- If men have no likeness to the Father in heaven, it is vain to talk of their being His "sons."
- If we know nothing of holiness we may flatter ourselves as we please, but we have not got the Holy Spirit dwelling in us:
- we are dead, and must be brought to life again
- we are lost, and must be found. **"As many as are led by the Spirit of God, they,"** **and they only,** **"are the sons of God."** *(Romans 8:14)* ~~(Rom. viii. 14.)~~
- We must show by our lives the family we belong to.
- We must let people ~~men~~ see by our good conversation that we are indeed the children of the Holy One, or our son-ship is but an empty name.
- "Say not," says Gurnall, "that thou hast royal blood in thy veins, and art born of God, except thou canst prove thy pedigree by daring to be holy."

We must be holy, because this is the most likely way to do good to others.

We cannot live to ourselves only in this world. Our lives will always be doing either good or harm to those who see them. They are a silent sermon which all can read. It is sad indeed when they are a sermon for the devil's cause, and not for God's. I believe that far more is done for Christ's kingdom by the holy living of believers than we are at all aware of.

There is a reality about such living which makes people ~~men~~ feel,

and requires ~~obliges~~ them to think. It carries a weight and influence with it which nothing else can give. It makes religion beautiful, and draws humans ~~men~~ to consider it, like a lighthouse seen afar off. The day of judgment will prove that many besides husbands have been won "without the word" by a holy life, *(1 Peter 3:1)* ~~(1 Pet. iii. 1.)~~

You may talk to persons about the doctrines of the Gospels, and few will listen, and still fewer understand. <u>But your life is an argument that none can escape.</u> There is a meaning about holiness which not even the most unlearned can help taking in. They may not understand justification, but they can understand charity.

I believe there is far more harm done by unholy and inconsistent Christians than we are aware of. Such people ~~men~~ are among Satan's best allies. They pull down by their lives what ministers build with their lips. They cause the chariot wheels of the Gospel to drive heavily. They supply the children of this world with a never ending excuse for remaining as they are.

- "I cannot see the use of so much religion," said an irreligious tradesman not long ago;

- "I observe that some of my customers are always talking about the Gospel, and faith, and election, and the blessed promises, and so forth; and yet these very people think nothing of cheating me of pence and half-pence, when they have an opportunity. Now, if religious persons can do such things, I do not see what good there is in religion."

I grieve to be obliged to write such things, but I fear that Christ's name is too often blasphemed because of the lives of Christians. Let us take heed lest the blood of souls should be required at our hands. From murder of souls by inconsistency and loose walking,

good Lord, deliver us! Oh, for the sake of others, if for no other reason, let us strive to be holy!

We must be holy, because our present comfort depends much upon it.

We cannot be too often reminded of this. We are sadly apt to forget that there is a close connection between

- <u>**sin and sorrow,**</u>
- <u>**holiness and happiness,**</u>
- <u>**sanctification and consolation.**</u>

SIN   SORROW   DEATH

God has so wisely ordered it, that our well-being and our well-doing are linked together. He has mercifully provided that even in this world it shall be peoples ~~man's~~ interest to be holy. Our justification is not by works

- our calling and election are not according to our works
- but it is vain for anyone to suppose that he will have a lively sense of his justification, or an assurance of his calling, so long as he neglects good works, or does not strive to live a holy life.
- **"Hereby we do know that we know Him, if we keep His commandments."** *(1 John 2:3)* ~~(1 John ii. 3)~~
- **"Hereby we know that we are of the truth, and shall assure our hearts."** *(1 John 2:19)* ~~(1 John iii. 19.)~~

A believer may as soon expect to feel the sun's rays upon a dark

and cloudy day, as to feel strong consolation in Christ while he does not follow Him fully. When the disciples forsook the Lord and fled, they escaped danger, but they were miserable and sad. When, shortly after, they confessed Him boldly before men, they were cast into prison and beaten; but we are told

"they rejoiced that they were counted worthy to suffer shame for His name." *(Acts 5:41)* (Acts v. 41.)

Oh, for our own sakes, if there were no other reason, let us strive to be holy! He that follows Jesus most fully will always follow Him most comfortably.

Lastly, we must be holy, because without holiness on earth we shall never be prepared to enjoy heaven. Heaven is a holy place.

The Lord of heaven is a holy Being. The angels are holy creatures. Holiness is written on everything in heaven. The book of Revelation says expressly,

"There shall in no wise enter into it anything that defileth, neither whatsoever worketh abomination, or maketh a lie." *(Revelation 21:27)* (Rev. xxi. 27.)

I appeal solemnly to everyone who reads these pages, <u>How shall we ever be at home and happy in heaven, if we die unholy?</u>

Death works no change. The grave makes no alteration. Each will rise again with the same character in which he breathed his last.

<u>Where will our place be if we are strangers to holiness now?</u>

Suppose for a moment that you were allowed to enter heaven without holiness.

- _What would you do?_

- ***What possible enjoyment could you feel there?***
- ***To which of all the saints would you join yourself, and by whose side would you sit down?***

Their pleasures are not your pleasures,

their tastes not your tastes,

their character not your character.

How could you possibly be happy, if you had not been holy on earth?

Now perhaps you love the company of the

- **light and the careless,**
- **the worldly minded and the covetous,**
- **the** partygoer **reveller and the pleasure-seeker,**
- **the ungodly and the profane.**

There will be none such in heaven.

Now perhaps you think the saints of God too strict and particular, and serious. You rather avoid them. You have no delight in their society. <u>There will be no other company in heaven.</u>

Now perhaps you think

- praying, and Scripture reading, and hymn singing, dull and melancholy, and stupid work a thing to be tolerated now and then, but not enjoyed.
- You reckon the Sabbath a burden and a weariness; you could not possibly spend more than a small part of it in worshipping God.

But remember, <u>heaven is a never-ending Sabbath</u>. The inhabitants thereof rest not day or night, saying, "***Holy, holy, holy, Lord God Almighty***" and singing the praise of the Lamb. <u>How could an unholy man find pleasure in occupation such as this?</u>

Think you that such an one would delight to meet David, and Paul, and John, after a life spent in doing the very things they spoke against?

Would he take sweet counsel with them, and find that he and they had much in common?

- Think you, above all, that he would rejoice to meet Jesus, the Crucified One, face to face, after cleaving to the sins for which He died, after loving His enemies and despising His friends?

- Would he stand before Him with confidence, and join in the cry, **"This is our God; we have waited for Him, we will be glad and rejoice in His salvation"**? *(Isaiah 25:9)* ~~(Isa. xxv. 9.)~~

- Think you not rather that the tongue of an unholy man would cleave to the roof of his mouth with shame, and his only desire would be to be cast out!

He would feel a stranger in a land he knew not, a black sheep amidst Christ's holy flock.

The voice of Cherubim and Seraphim, the song of Angels and Archangels and all the company of heaven, would be a language he could not understand. The very air would seem an air he could not breathe. I know not what others may think, but to me it does seem clear that

heaven would be a miserable place to an unholy man.

It cannot be otherwise. People may say, in a vague way, "they hope to go to heaven;" but they do not consider what they say. There must be a certain "meetness for the inheritance of the saints in light." Our hearts must be somewhat in tune. To reach the holiday of glory, we must pass through the training school of grace. We must be heavenly-minded, and have heavenly tastes, in the life that now is, or else we shall never find ourselves in heaven, in the life to come.

And now, before I go any further, let me say a few words by way of application.

For one thing, let me ask everyone who may read these pages,

Are you holy?

Listen, I pray you, to the question I put to you this day.

Do you know anything of the holiness of which I have been speaking?

- I do not ask whether you attend your church regularly
- whether you have been baptized, and received the Lord's Supper
- whether you have the name of Christian

I ask something more than all this:

Are you holy, or are you not?

I do not ask whether you
- approve of holiness in others
- whether you like to read the lives of holy people,
- and to talk of holy things,
- and to have on your table holy books
- whether you mean to be holy,
- and hope you will be holy some day

 I ask something further:

Are you yourself holy this very day, or are you not?

And why do I ask so straitly, and press the question so strongly? I do it because the Scripture says, "**Without holiness no man shall see the Lord.**" It is written, it is not my fancy

- it is the Bible, not my private opinion
- it is the word of God, not of man

- **"Without holiness no man shall see the Lord."** *(Hebrews 12:14)* ~~(Heb. xii. 14.)~~

Alas, what searching, sifting words are these! What thoughts come across my mind, as I write them down!

I look at the world, and see the greater part of it lying in wickedness.

I look at professing Christians, and see the vast majority having nothing of Christianity but the name.

I turn to the Bible, and I hear the Spirit saying, "Without holiness no man shall see the Lord."

Surely it is a text that ought to make us consider our ways, and search our hearts. <u>Surely it should raise within us solemn thoughts, and send us to prayer.</u>

You may try to put me off by saying **"you feel much, and think much about these things: far more than many suppose."**

I answer, **"This is not the point.** The poor lost souls in hell do as much as this. The great question is not what you think, and what you feel, but what you do."

You may say, **"It was never meant that all Christians should be holy, and that holiness, such as I have described, is only for great saints, and people of uncommon gifts."**

I answer, "I cannot see that in Scripture. I read that every man who hath hope in Christ purifieth himself." *(1 John 3:3)* ~~(1 John iii. 3.)~~

"Without holiness no man shall see the Lord."

You may say, **"It is impossible to be so holy and to do our duty in this life at the same time: the thing cannot be done."**

I answer, "You are mistaken. It can be done. With Christ on your side nothing is impossible. It has been done by many. David, and Obadiah, and Daniel, and the servants of Nero's household, are all examples that go to prove it."

NOTHING IS IMPOSSIBLE WITH GOD.
- LUKE 1:37

You may say, "**If I were so holy I would be unlike other people.**"

I answer, "I know it well. It is just what you ought to be. Christ's true servants always were unlike the world around them

- a separate nation, a peculiar people;

- and you must be so too, if you would be saved!"

You may say, "**At this rate very few will be saved.**"

I answer, "**I know it. It is precisely what we are told in the Sermon on the Mount.**"

The Lord Jesus said so 1,900 years ago.

- "How narrow is the gate and the way is restricted that leads to life! There are few who find it" *(Matthew 7:14)* "~~Strait is the gate, and narrow is the way, that leadetn unto life, and few there be that find it." (Matt. vii. 14.)~~

- Few will be saved, because few will take the trouble to seek salvation.

People ~~Men~~ will not deny themselves the pleasures of sin and their own way for a little season. They turn their backs on an "inheritance incorruptible, undefiled, and that fate ~~fadeth~~ not away."

"**Ye will not come unto Me,**" says Jesus, "**that ye might have life.**" *(John 5:40)* ~~(John v. 40.)~~

You may say, "**These are hard sayings: the way is very narrow.**" I answer, "I know it. So says the Sermon on the Mount." The Lord Jesus said so 1,900 years ago.

He always said that people ~~men~~

- must take up the cross daily,

- and that they must be ready to cut off hand or foot, if they would be His disciples.

It is in religion as it is in other things, **"there are no gains without pains."** That which costs nothing is worth nothing.

Whatever we may think fit to say, we must be holy, if we would see the Lord. Where is our Christianity if we are not? We must not merely have a Christian name, and Christian knowledge, we must have a Christian character also. We must be saints on earth, if ever we mean to be saints in heaven.

God has said it, and He will not go back: **"Without holiness no man shall see the Lord."**

"The Pope's calendar," says Jenkyn, **"only makes saints of the dead, but Scripture <u>requires sanctity in the living</u>."**

"Let not people ~~men~~ deceive themselves," says Owen; "sanctification is a qualification indispensably necessary unto those who will be under the conduct of the Lord Christ unto salvation. <u>He leads none to heaven but whom He sanctifies on the earth.</u> <u>This living Head will not admit of **dead members**.</u>"

Surely we need not wonder that Scripture says **"Ye must be born again."** *(John 3:7)* (John iii. 7.) Surely it is clear as noon-day that many professing Christians need a complete change

- new hearts, new natures if ever they are to be saved.

- Old things must pass away they must become new creatures.

" **Without holiness no person** ~~man~~," be whom ~~he who~~ they ~~he~~ may, **"shall see the Lord."**

Let me, for another thing, speak a little to believers. I ask you this question, <u>"Do you think you feel the importance of holiness as much as you should?"</u>

I own I fear the temper of the times about this subject. I doubt exceedingly whether it holds that place which it deserves in the thoughts and attention of some of the Lord's people. I would humbly suggest that we are apt to overlook the doctrine of growth in grace, and that we do not sufficiently consider how very far a person may go in a profession of religion, and yet have no grace, and be dead in God's sight after all.

I believe that Judas Iscariot seemed very like the other Apostles. When the Lord warned them that one would betray Him, no one said, "Is it Judas?" We had better think more about the Churches of Sardis and Laodicea than we do.

I have no desire to make an idol of holiness.

I do not wish to dethrone Christ, and put holiness in His place. But I must candidly say, I wish sanctification was more thought of in this day than it seems to be, and I therefore take occasion to press the subject on all believers into whose hands these pages may fall. I fear it is sometimes forgotten that God has married together justification and sanctification. They are distinct and different things, beyond question, but one is never found without the other.

All justified people are sanctified, and all sanctified are justified.

What God has joined together let no person ~~man~~ dare to put into pieces ~~asunder~~. Tell me not of your justification, unless you have also some marks of sanctification.

Boast not of Christ's work for you, unless you can show us the Spirit's work in you. Think not that Christ and the Spirit can ever be divided.

I doubt not that many believers know these things, but I think it good for us to be put in remembrance of them. Let us prove that we know them by our lives. Let us try to keep in view this text more continually: "**Follow holiness, without which no person ~~man~~ shall see the Lord.**"

I must frankly say I wish there was not such an excessive sensi-
tiveness on the subject of holiness as I sometimes perceive in the
minds of believers. A person ~~man~~
might really think it was a dangerous subject to handle, so cautiously
is it touched! Yet surely when we
have exalted Christ as **"the way,
the truth, and the life,"** we cannot error ~~err~~ in speaking strongly
about what should be the character
of His people.

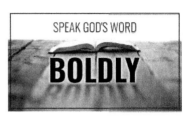

Well says Rutherford, "The way that carries ~~erieth~~ down duties
and sanctification, is not the way of grace. Believing and doing are
blood-friends."

I would say it with all reverence, but say it I must

- I sometimes fear if Christ were on earth now, there are not a few
  who would think His preaching legal;

- and if Paul were writing his Epistles, there are those who would
  think he had better not write the latter? art of most of them as he
  did.

<u>But let us remember that the Lord Jesus did speak the Sermon on
the Mount, and that the Epistle to the Ephesians contains six
chapters and not four. I grieve to feel obliged to speak in this way,
but I am sure there is a cause.</u>

That great divine, John Owen, the Dean of Christ Church, used to
say, more than two hundred years ago, that there were people
<u>whose whole religion seemed to consist in going about complain-
ing of their own corruptions, and telling everyone that they could
do nothing of themselves</u>. I am
afraid that after two centuries the
same thing might be said with
truth of some of Christ's professing
people in this day.

I know there are texts in Scripture
which warrant such complaints. I
do not object to them when they come from people ~~men~~ who walk

in the steps of the Apostle Paul, and <u>fight a good fight</u>, as he did, against sin, the devil, and the world. But I never like such complaints when I see ground for suspecting, as I often do, <u>that they are only a cloak to cover</u> **spiritual laziness**, and an <u>excuse for</u> **spiritual sloth**.

If we say with Paul, "**O wretched man that I am**," let us also be able to say with him, "**I press toward the mark**." Let us not quote his example in one thing, while we do not follow him in another. *(Romans 7:24) (Philippians 3:14)* ~~(Rom. vii. 24; Philip. iii. 14.)~~

I do not set up myself to be better than other people, and if anyone asks, "**What are you, that you write in this way**?"

I answer, "<u>I am a very poor creature indeed</u>." But I say that I cannot read the Bible without desiring to see many believers

- more spiritual,

- more holy,

- more single-eyed,

- more heavenly-minded,

- more whole-hearted than they are in the nineteenth century.

I want to see among believers more of a pilgrim spirit, a

- more decided separation from the world,

- a conversation more evidently in heaven,

- a closer walk with God

- and therefore I have written as I have.

Is it not true that we need a higher standard of personal holiness in this day?

Where is out patience?

Where is our zeal?

Where is our love?

Where are our works?

Where is the power of religion to be seen, as it was in times gone by?

Where is that unmistakable tone which used to distinguish the saints of old, and shake the world?

Verily our silver has become dross, our wine mixed with water, and our salt has very little flavor ~~savour~~.

We are all more than half asleep. The night is far spent, and the day is at hand. Let us awake, and sleep no more.

Let us open our eyes more widely than we have done previously ~~hitherto~~.

- "Therefore let's also, seeing we are surrounded by so great a cloud of witnesses, lay aside every weight and the sin which so easily entangles us, and let's run with perseverance the race that is set before us," *(Romans 7:24)*

- ~~"Let us lay aside every weight, and the sin that doth so easily beset us."(Heb. xii. i)~~

- "Let us cleanse ourselves from all filthiness of flesh and spirit, and perfect holiness in the fear of God." *(2 Corinthians 7:1)* ~~(2 Cor. vii. 1.)~~

- "Did Christ die," says Owen, "and shall sin live?

- Was He crucified in the world, and shall our affections to the world be quick and lively? Oh, where is the spirit of him, who by the cross of Christ was crucified to the world, and the world to him!"

Let me, in the last place, offer a word of advice to all who desire to be holy.

Would you be holy? Would you become a new creature?

Then you must begin with Christ. You will do just nothing at all, and make no progress till you feel your sin and weakness, and flee to Him. He is the root and beginning of all holiness, and the way to be holy is to come to Him by faith and be joined to Him.

Christ is not wisdom and righteousness only to His people, but sanctification also. People ~~Men~~ sometimes try to make themselves holy first of all, and sad work they make of it. They toil and labor ~~labour~~, and turn over new leaves, and make many changes; and yet, like the woman with the issue of blood, before she came to Christ, they feel "nothing bettered, but rather worse." *(Mark 5:26)*

(Mark v. 26.)

-They run in vain, and labor labour in vain; and little wonder, for they are beginning at the wrong end.

-They are building up a wall of sand; their work runs down as fast as they throw it up.

-They are baling water out of a leaky vessel: the leak gains on them, not they on the leak.

Other foundation of "holiness" can no human man lay than that which Paul laid, even Christ Jesus. "I am the vine. You are the branches. He who remains in me and I in him bears much fruit, for apart from me you can do nothing." *(John 15:5)*

"Without Christ we can do nothing." (John xv. 5.)

It is a strong but true saying of Traill's, "Wisdom out of Christ is damning folly

- righteousness out of Christ is guilt and condemnation

- sanctification out of Christ is filth and sin

- redemption out of Christ is bondage and slavery."

Do you want to attain holiness?

Do you feel this day a real hearty desire to be holy?

Would you be a partaker of the Divine nature?

Then go to Christ.

Wait for nothing.

Wait for nobody.

 Linger not.

Think not to make yourself ready. Go and say to Him, in the words of that beautiful hymn - Nothing in my hand I bring, Simply to Thy cross I cling; Naked, flee to Thee for dress; Helpless, look to Thee for grace.

There is not a brick nor a stone laid in the work of our sanctification till we go to Christ. Holiness is His special gift to His believing people. Holiness is the work He carries on in their hearts, by the Spirit whom He puts within them.

He is appointed a "Prince and a Savior ~~Saviour~~, to give repentance" as well as remission of sins.

- "To as many as receive Him, He gives power to become sons of God." *(Acts 5:31) (John 1:12-13)* ~~(Acts v. 31; John i. 12, 13.)~~ Holiness comes not of blood

- parents cannot give it to their children: nor yet of the will of the flesh

- people ~~man~~ cannot produce it in themselves ~~himself~~: nor yet of the will of humans ~~man~~

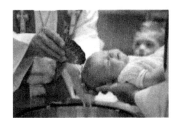

- ministers cannot give it you by baptism.

<u>Holiness comes from Christ.</u> It is the result of vital union with Him, It is the fruit of being a living branch of the True Vine.

Go then to Christ and say, ***"Lord, not only save me from the guilt of sin, but send the Spirit, whom Thou didst promise, and save me from its power. Make me holy. Teach me to do Thy will**."*

Would you continue holy?

Then abide in Christ. He says Himself, **"Abide in Me and I in you, - he that abideth in Me and I in him, the same beareth much fruit**." *(John 15:4-5)* ~~(John xv. 4, 5.)~~

- It pleased the Father that in Him should all fulness dwell - a full supply for all a believer's wants.

- He is the Physician to whom you must daily go, if you would keep well.

- He is the Manna which you must daily eat, and the Rock of which you must daily drink.

- His arm is the arm on which you must daily lean, as you come up out of the wilderness of this world.

- You must not only be rooted, you must also be built up in Him.

Paul was a man of God indeed

-a holy man

-a growing, thriving Christian

-and what was the secret of it all? He was one to whom Christ was **"all in all."**

-He was ever **"looking unto Jesus."**

-**"I can do all things,"** he says, **"through Christ which strengthened me."**

-**"I live, yet not I, but Christ liveth in me. The life that I now live, I live by the faith of the Son of God."**

Let us go and do likewise. *(Hebrew 12:2) (Philippians 4:13) (Galatians 2:20)* ~~(Heb. xii. 2; Phil. iv. 13; Gal. ii. 20.)~~

May all who read these pages know these things by experience, and not by hearsay only.

May we all feel the importance of holiness, far more than we have ever done yet!

May our years be holy years with our souls, and then they will be happy ones!

Whether we live, may we live unto the Lord; or whether we die, may we die unto the Lord; of if He comes for us, may we be found in peace, without spot, and blameless!

Printed in Great Britain
by Amazon